Awakening Mind

Travels with my Self

John C. Seniff

Copyright © 2007 by John C. Seniff

All rights reserved. No part of this book shall be reproduced or transmitted in any form or by any means, electronic, mechanical, magnetic, photographic including photocopying, recording or by any information storage and retrieval system, without prior written permission of the publisher. No patent liability is assumed with respect to the use of the information contained herein. Although every precaution has been taken in the preparation of this book, the publisher and author assume no responsibility for errors or omissions. Neither is any liability assumed for damages resulting from the use of the information contained herein.

ISBN 0-7414-3811-9

Cover photo copyright by John C. Seniff.

Author photo copyright by Kelly E. Kishbaugh.

John C. Seniff
revpuresound@hotmail.com

Published by:

1094 New DeHaven Street, Suite 100
West Conshohocken, PA 19428-2713
Info@buybooksontheweb.com
www.buybooksontheweb.com
Toll-free (877) BUY BOOK
Local Phone (610) 941-9999
Fax (610) 941-9959

Printed in the United States of America

Printed on Recycled Paper

Published March 2007

Thanks to Ashley, Mary, Connie, Kelly, and especially my companion Cruz who is here with me always in Spirit after passing away on my birthday May 25, 2005.

Contents

1. The Beginning — 1
2. In the Presence of A Zen Master — 3
3. Land of Enchantment — 11
4. The Grange — 24
5. Close Encounters in Alabama — 33
6. On A Mission from Buddha — 36
7. Down into the Canyon — 42
8. Balls of Light — 50
9. The Vineyard — 53
10. Moving On — 60
11. Mary — 67
12. Journey to India — 74
13. The Raven — 86
14. A True Companion — 91
15. Keeping on the Path — 103
16. Face-off with Nature — 107
17. Trusting Your Gut — 110
18. Getting Centered — 113
19. Raising Big Mind — 115

20. Study With A Zen Master	121
21. The "Proposal"	131
22. Entering the Rank of Buddha	136
23. However and Whatever	143
24. A Return to India	147
25. Epilogue	153

You should love him as he is a non-God, a non-spirit, a non-person, a non-image, but as he is a pure, unmixed, bright "One," separated from all duality; and in that One we should eternally sink down, out of "something" into "nothing".

May God help us to do that. Amen.

Meister Eckhart

The Beginning

There is a photograph of me as a young child sitting on the tractor with my Uncle Edwin who has a pipe hanging from his mouth. It was 1958 on a hot Alabama day. This was the Deep South. Humidity wrapped around you like a moist blanket. Sometimes if the breeze hit you just right, you felt caressed by Mother Nature herself.

All of one's senses are activated and through the senses this extraordinary thing called Life. A beckoning towards something that seems endless and eternal. But what is that?

For now, a slice of watermelon while rocking on the porch eases the deep thoughts and the mind is free to wander onto the fields and sky. Today is today. Yesterday is yesterday. Tomorrow is tomorrow.

The religion of my grandparents left nothing to the imagination. Though it gave them something on which to lean, to depend, it seemed chaotic and unsure—like people getting into emotional turmoil for Jesus. Jesus was the answer and there was no room for questions. This did not fit in with my nature religion. I, of course, had not given it any name, but I felt it and knew something was there.

When I turned eight, our family moved to India. My stepfather was working for the State Department.

This was the first time I began to recognize something of human form and creation coinciding with what I was beginning to see. The world of India was completely different. Unlike the sterility and boredom of the Baptist churches, Temples and *stupas* were full of intrigue and mystery.

After spending a few years in India, we moved to Thailand, the Philippines and finally to England where I graduated from high school. It was in England that my mind continued to expand. I read and read, questioned and questioned, from politics to psychology to religion.

The Beginning

One day I was introduced to a book called *The Way of Zen* by Alan Watts. I couldn't put it down. There was something about Zen Buddhism that spoke directly to me.

The flower opens and the world arises

Chuandeng lu 3

My wish was to meet an authentic Zen Master.

In the Presence of A Zen Master

Having a mind neither stilled nor disturbed in the presence of all things in the environment, neither concentrated nor distracted, passing through all sound and form without lingering or obstruction is called being a wayfarer.

Pai-chang

A telephone call from my cousin in Annapolis, Maryland announces that a Zen Master has been interviewed in the "Washington Post." He apparently lives nearby, so I hurriedly write to the "Washington Post" to request his address in order to meet him. Then it occurs to me that maybe...just maybe, he is listed in the telephone book and he is.

Grasping the phone and with a nervous voice and trembling knees, I speak first to his wife, an American.

She sounds friendly. "Yes, I would be happy to get him."

I wait quietly staring anxiously out at the Chesapeake Bay.

"Herro!"

"Ah...yes...Reverend.... My name is John...and...well...I was wondering if you...I mean, if I...could meet with you sometime. I saw your interview in the Post."

"Ah...yes...so-so-so! Hmmmm, good. Yah, sure! I get wife to tell directions...OK?"

"Thank you yes...." Handing back the phone, she gives me directions to a place called Deerwood, in Maryland.

This was it. I was now actually going to talk with a real life in-the-flesh Zen Master! It felt as though I had achieved a little enlightenment or mini "*satori*" just from getting in touch with him.

Two days later I found myself in his home office drinking green tea. I could feel a strong force coming from him. He struck me as "goodness" itself, "beauty" itself. Maybe the robes had something to do with it, but no...it was more than that. There was something about this man, to be sure.

He asked basic questions. "What do I do?" "Where are my parents?" "What does my father do?" "When did I learn of Zen?" We talk a little about meditation, he told me of his dislike for TM (transcendental meditation). "You might as well hit yourself over the head with a hammer to get the same results! Meditation is a dynamic thing, not a dead thing."

After about an hour's talk punctuated with long pauses, he invited me to stay for lunch. At lunch he was in a more jovial mood. His laugh was childlike and I found myself getting caught up in his humor, a mixture of wit and slapstick.

A few days later I went back and we discussed my training. He invited me to live with him saying that his wife liked me and was comfortable with me being in the same house. I was flattered by the invitation, but also a little nervous. To live in a friend's house is one thing, but to live under the same roof with one's teacher twenty four hours a day, is quite another.

My mother, was not especially pleased, feeling that this was drawing me away from what she felt were my Christian roots. At the same time she was having problems with my stepfather. It looked like they were going to divorce and she was very worried about her security and future. I suggested that she talk to Zenji (Zen teacher).

A few days later, sitting on his couch, my mother was trying to be strong, but eventually broke into tears. Both of us sat quietly and then after a few minutes Zenji spoke up saying that it was a good thing at this time for her to support her son.

"Your son is doing a great thing now. His desire is to be a mature and intelligent man, rather than a person led by only worldly and relative matters. You need to look happily at your son's future now, and not only be concerned with your own situation."

She raised her head slightly, looked over at me, and then glanced at him. I was surprised and gratified by what he had to say. He seemed not only to grasp what my mother needed to hear, but also what I needed to hear. Never had I felt someone being such an advocate for me. Tears welled up in my eyes.

My parents divorced, and my mother moved to Tallahassee, Florida. I moved in with Zenji and began my training. Mike, the senior student, lived next door. Ten years older than me, he had met Zenji in New York City while on pilgrimage. At the time, Mike was deeply concerned about the question of death. Approaching one of the Zen Centers, they told him that there was no resident Zen Master, except this mendicant priest sleeping in the loft. Mike and Zenji hit it off immediately and Mike had been with him off and on ever since. Zenji referred to Mike mostly as "stupid Mike," to the point that I felt bad for him. I would later learn that Mike could be quite pushy and irritating. Being a hard worker and meticulous, he would scold me or "get on my case," whenever I got lazy or lax. I could see Zenji's reasoning, but on the whole I found him to be a "pain in the butt Mike!"

Sitting meditation was two hours in the morning and evening unless we planned something else. One day the three of us went out and bought a Ping-Pong table. We played for hours on end, usually making bets with food, sweets mostly. These were some of the most enjoyable times for me because this is also a way to study Zen. As it says in the Heart Sutra, "Form is emptiness and emptiness is form." There are many ways to study and learn, not just one or a few. Forms are numerous and through forms with Right Understanding, one can perceive and connect with the Universal or Buddha-nature. So even a game (or in this case, many games) can lead one to that. As I began to understand this, the image of a silent and stoic Zen monk or student striving for enlightenment was beginning to evaporate. Pain as well as joy is all part of it; nothing divided, nothing separated.

Our daily routine was comprised of clearing the forest area, planting a garden, building a rock garden, making trips to get manure, digging up bamboo shoots, landscaping, taking walks or short road trips and then talks or lectures which could go late into the evening. Zenji was also always testing us. One day he told me to try to talk the man next door into opening up a couple of bottles of wine from his cellar and sharing them with us.

"But when you approach him, bow to him and kneel on the cement until he says yes."

Mike and Zenji waited smoking their cigarettes while I approached him. Reluctantly, I followed Zenji's instructions exactly. The man, named Jack was both astonished and somewhat embarrassed—but no more than I was.

"Oh...uh...wine? Uh...yeah...sure. Right now?" backing up slightly.

"No...not now, but later. This evening maybe."

How about seven then?"

"Yes...good." Getting up I hurried back to the house. Zenji seemed pleased and said, "Good, good, this is nice for us John, but actually very nice for him."

It was true. That evening, I could see that Jack, a bachelor, was quite happy to have our company and share his wine. He had a guitar, so I played some music and then Jack wanted to show us a few magic tricks. All of us got a little intoxicated and after the party we walked home slowly, to Zenji's singing of traditional Japanese folk tunes.

Another time, I was chopping some small branches off a log while Mike, who was behind me, was cutting down a large tree with a chain saw. The tree was ready to fall but Zenji told me to continue working and not to mind it. Mike stopped sawing and the tree stood there not moving. I was getting progressively nervous. Then Zenji started telling me something about Jesus and his disciples and their reluctance to step over the boat to walk on water, obviously indicating something about trust.

I tried to push myself to get beyond a certain place of letting go of my fear and concentrating on my work. Once I was able to do that, he went over and gave the tree a push. I moved out of the way, but when it came down it fell quite near, just missing me. Zenji giggled and looked at me with a big beaming smile. I glanced at him with a nervous smile. "How about a beer and Ping-Pong?" he said. "Beer...did I hear beer?" I thought, still feeling nervous. "Yeah...I could definitely use one right now!"

We also had koan study. I was given the question; "Does a dog have Buddha-nature?" "Yes...no...not sure...possibly...yes everything has God or Buddha in it...of course...depends on if you like the dog or not...etc. etc." I learned to chant and later to memorize the Heart Sutra. It amazed me, that while I consciously remembered only a couple of lines –one day I woke up knowing the whole thing!

Zenji's personality adapted quickly to situations or persons. He had many facets yet also remained true to his nature. He could be calm and at the same time quite passionate, and was free in expression of his anger, joy or sadness.

I not only learned so much from what he said, but also just by watching him. There was no separation between words and behavior, and he approached everything with impeccability.

One late afternoon Zenji and his wife Barbara and I were sitting out on the back porch drinking tea and eating Japanese snacks. I noticed that Zenji was staring up at the clouds. They were like large floating cotton balls, tinged with orange, passing over the treetops.

"Did you know John that you can ride clouds?"

"You can?" somewhat puzzled. "How?" I looked over at Barbara and she looked at me with a serene smile.

"You can, if you wish," he responded looking directly into my eyes. His eyes seemed to glimmer.

"Yes I would love to!"

Looking up at the clouds, "Then go there with your mind."

> *Like a drifting cloud,*
> *Bound by nothing:*
> *I just let go*
> *Giving myself up*
> *To the whim of the wind.*
> Zen Priest Ryokan

Whack, whack, whack, and whack! On one side of my back and then the other side. Flying into splintered particles, the pinewood *kysaku* (the disciplinary/wake up stick used in Zen monasteries) can't endure the impact of the beatings my Zen Master is giving me. But this is more than a wake up call. Second stick. Whack! Four times on each side of the back. This time I flinch a little, feeling the sting going ever deeper into my flesh and muscles. From the corner of my eye I see him perfectly execute the direction of the stick with the full force of his body. It splinters all over the *zendo* (meditation room). Now holding half of the stick, he walks over to the senior student and inflicts him with the same number of strikes. Then he drops what's left of the *kyasku* and walks out. Mike and I quietly pick up the small pieces of wood from the floor.

After cleaning the *zendo*, I go to the bathroom and look in the mirror. Streaks of blue, purple and black with tiny cuts of blood have formed on each side of my spine. Washing off, it hurts to put my shirt back on. I walk into my teacher's study where he is immersed in a book and drinking tea. He looks up at me and asks if I'd like tea, I say "Yes."

Sitting on the couch I'm not sure what to say at first, but then I tell him "Thank you," though I'm not sure why. He nods his head and looks at me kindly. Together in silence, we sit looking out the window.

> *Anybody can enter Buddha's world*
> *So few can step into the Devil's*
> Zen Priest Ikkyu

I am riding on a horse that is jumping over fences. Going through a pasture, through a beautiful green land, similar to the area around England. I get off the horse in this beautiful area, and standing there next to me is another me, that looks like me. I begin to tell this other me how to ride the horse and explain what to do. The other me gets on the horse and takes off. I decide to walk on. I feel thirsty, and as I continue walking through these beautiful rolling hills, I find myself at an outside patio with water gushing out from a beautiful fountain in the middle. Finely dressed people are standing all around in what appears to be a very luxurious cocktail party. The women in their jewelry and fine clothes, and the men in their tuxedos

I have no desire to join any of this. Instead I go and sit down beside the fountain, and because I am thirsty, I reach out to scoop up some water from the fountain. Just as I am about to do that, I hear a quiet but very powerful voice, says to me, "Drink from me." Looking over I see a tree -- A very simple tree with a big trunk and leaves around it. It is like looking into another dimension. The tree is glowing with a gold, yellow light all around it. Again it repeats, "Come drink from me." I stand up and start walking toward it. I feel I have stepped into another dimension and everything else is gone. As I stand there in front of the tree, it starts dripping liquid from its bark. Again it says to me, "Drink from me." This time I feel the voice coming from within me, much more powerfully. Reaching up my finger, I take a bit of a drop and taste it. It has a nice taste--like sweet honey water. Then the voice says to me, "There's more where this comes from." I look down and see a little stream at the base of the tree being formed, flowing out into the country.

I kneel down on one knee, and look in my hand, and there in my hand is a chalice, a grail. I start to dip the chalice in the water to drink from it.

I awake.

Land of Enchantment

After a while I left Zenji. After having the tree dream, I made my first trip to Abiquiu, New Mexico, wanting to explore my Christian roots. Why, I'm not sure, but something had begun to frighten me internally. Perhaps I was losing that sense of familiarity with my surroundings and who I thought I was. The reality with which I identified was beginning to fragment.

I was making a journey to Christ in the Desert Monastery to participate in an experimental Benedictine community called "The Grange." It was to be a smaller community, connected to Mt. Saviour Monastery in New York, but separate in its practice from the larger monastery. Men and women would participate, and there would be the study of other traditions east and west.

After spending a couple of weeks with my friend Ken in Lincoln, Nebraska, I hopped a Greyhound bus and headed towards New Mexico, passing through Wyoming and Colorado. A couple of days later I arrived in Espanola, New Mexico, a small mostly Hispanic town, about 45 minutes from Abiquiu. The bus station was an old looking white adobe structure. I was hoping to get a ride from a girl that I had met on the bus, but when her mother came to pick her up, she looked at me suspiciously and said "No." So, that was that. Heading out towards the main road, I postured myself for a ride. A drunken young man driving a pick up truck pulled over. As I tried to find room among the beer cans for my feet, he politely asked if I'd like a beer. I said "Thank you, but no," hoping to not have to listen to his ramblings. No such luck! He was bent on talking about his wife and how domineering she was...needless to say, his reason for drinking.

"Yaah man! Women...can't live with them, can't shoot 'em. The few months its romantic and stuff...and then one day you awake wondering how that hyena got in your bed!"

Downing another beer he flings it within inches of my face and out the window. At one point we careened off the road. Thanks only to the open land we avoided collision. At last we reached Abiquiu. Getting out of the truck I wish him luck. Glassy-eyed, he tips his hat to me and wishes me the same.

It was getting late and I wanted to call the "family" (friends of the monastery) to see if they could get in touch with one of the monks to come and pick me up. The monastery was way off the beaten track, thirteen miles down the bottom of a canyon to be precise, and their only means of communication was via walkie-talkies. I had no luck getting in touch with anyone. They knew I was coming but maybe they had "closing" hours, who knew?

The choices were to either hitch hike up the road, or to prop myself up next to the general store and get some sleep, hoping that someone would eventually come along to pick me up. Cars on this road were few and far between—especially at this hour, so I opted for the latter. Pulling out my guitar, I serenaded the night and then fell asleep curled up next to my knapsack and guitar.

Around midnight a man in a white pick-up truck pulled up to the phone booth to call his daughter in Nebraska. When he had finished, he asked if I needed a lift anywhere.

"Do you happen to know where Christ in the Desert Monastery is?"

"Hmm...I've heard of it. Maybe someone at Ghost Ranch knows... Are you a monk?"

"Well, not quite yet, but you could say I'm a beginning monk." I went on to explain my interest in monasticism as a way of life and of spiritual practice rather as a means of devoting myself to a particular religion.

I wasn't sure what we would discover from the abandoned saloons and tumbleweeds on the drive towards Ghost Ranch, which I later learned was a conference and retreat center run by the Presbyterians—a white man's Pueblo of sorts.

Along the road towards the ranch there were no lights on in any of the adobe homes, though a little farther did we finally see a single home with a light on in the living room. We stopped, and the driver knocked on the door while I stayed in the truck. A slim, wiry elderly woman soon opened it. She was naturally suspicious to be faced with strangers at her door at that hour and questioned us sternly as to what we wanted.

"We're looking for the monastery that's supposed to be around this area. Do you happen to know where it is?" Meanwhile I just sat in the truck wondering what this elderly lady was doing out here in the middle of nowhere. Reluctantly she gave us directions and then said in a scolding tone, "But don't go bothering those monks!" Turning around my driving companion retorted, "Lady...this man *is* a monk." She quickly apologized as we pulled quietly out of her driveway. She stood there watching us till we were out of sight.

Turning to me he said, "You know who I think that was?"

"No."

"Georgia O'Keefe."

"Georgia who?" I asked. He went on to explain that she was a famous artist who had come to New Mexico years ago and that this area had contributed a lot to her creativity.

"I thought she was dead."

"Well, I guess not, unless we just saw a ghost." We both chuckled. Hispanics once called this area, and maybe they still do, "El Rancho de Los Brujos"---the "Ranch of the Witches."

Leaving Ghost Ranch, I began to have the feeling of participating in a dream. It was like the time when, at the age of nine, I moved from a small southern town in Florida to New Delhi, India. Arriving at four in the morning at the international airport, we were driven down a narrow and winding road through a progression of cows, water buffalo and men all wearing white. The only traffic was bicycles veering off in all directions to avoid us. The buildings themselves had odd formations, spiraling peaks that looked liked Dairy Queen cones, and there were sculptures of

Land of Enchantment

animals and women whose breasts were so large and well proportioned that I couldn't begin to take my eyes off them.

As we began our descent into the canyon I had that similar feeling—again I was a stranger in a strange land. And yet, it was different. This time I was thrown way back in time—before man, to the time of the dinosaurs, when rock formations looked like odd alien beings. The stars themselves were so bright it was as though I was viewing a completely different galaxy. It was the same planet, yet planets and skies never seen this way before. Here there was no pollution. There was neither the disturbance of environment nor the disturbance of perception. In that moment, a sense of clarity and newness arose in me that felt like a supernova about to explode.

I gestured for him to stop so I could relieve the intensity of bodily fluids. My driving companion got out of the truck and breathed in deeply.

"Do you smell that?" I thought it might have been me.

"There is nothing like breathing the fresh air." I nodded while looking casually up in the sky. He was right, so right, but there was also a slightly perfumed scent here that I learned later came from the high desert sage.

Getting back into the truck we drove on for a couple of miles or so and then...

"Do you hear that?"

"Hear what?

"That!" We sat there until finally the sound emerged in my ears. It was the sound of water, the last thing I expected to hear in this terrain. It felt like a muffled voice beckoning from the distance.

"That's the Chama River or "Mud River" if you want translate in English. Nature sure doesn't let you forget who or what you are."

I began to realize that this man had been sent to me—an angel, a Bodhisattva, or simply, just a human being like the rest of us. In any case, one who had not lost touch with the real world. All I knew for sure was that he was a middle-aged man from Nebraska that owned a white Ford pick-up truck. It didn't seem important to know of our family histories, occupations, or hobbies.

We finally reached the monastery at the bottom of the canyon. Passing through the entrance gate, we continued a quarter of a mile until reaching the guesthouse. With the engine turned off, we sat quietly there and surveyed the territory. I was sad that this part of the journey was over. I thanked him and told him that I hoped he would come and visit me. He turned and looking directly at me and he said, "The best thanks you can give yourself and others is to be true to Who You Are. If you are to be a monk, do it for others and not just for yourself."

The impact of his words struck me like a meteorite on the back of my head. I sat there quietly before shaking his hand and tried to force a smile through a sudden mix of emotions. Slowly I got out of his truck and he departed. Watching him disappear around the bend and towards the river, I felt alone.

When I turned around I saw the figure of a person coming towards me carrying a kerosene lamp. She appeared to be wearing nun's clothing.

"You must be John? I was expecting you tonight."

I thought to myself... "How did she know I was coming?" I had never reached anyone. "How did she know it was me, specifically, and not someone else?" She took me to a small adobe room, which was no larger than a monk's cell or a large walk-in closet. She lit the kerosene lamp, which was sitting on a small wooden desk.

"I hope this will be comfortable for you. If you are cold, there is a stack of wood along the wall outside." Her voice was soft and the words seemed to float in mid-air before reaching my ears.

I thanked her and she gave me a hug. The gesture surprised me.

"Sleep well." In what seemed like a ghostly form, she left casting shadows within the walls of my room.

It felt good to be in my cell. I was tired but energized. A fire in the small adobe fireplace would be a welcome friend, so I gathered some wood from outside and put in a few logs. The smell of *pinon* wood filled the room like incense. I stretched out on the Navaho rug and stared at the flames, deep in thought about my driving companion and his parting words. The more I thought about them, the deeper they sank into me. He had seemed so simple, yet it was more and more apparent that he was someone of substance.

Getting into bed, I pulled out a book by Meister Eckhart a 14th century Christian theologian and philosopher. He seemed to support the very words I had just heard.

> *Human beings ought to communicate*
> *And share*
> *All the gifts they have received from God.*
> *If a person has something that she does not*
> *share with others*
> *That person is not good.*
> *A person who does not bestow on others*
> *Spiritual things*
> *And the joy that is in them*
> *Has in fact never been spiritual.*
> *People are not to receive*
> *And keep gifts for themselves alone*
> *But should share themselves*
> *And pour forth everything they possess*
> *As much as possible.*

There was a knock at the door of my room.

"Come in!" barely awake I pushed myself up from the pillow.

An older man wearing a monk's habit walked in.

"You must be John? I'm glad to see you made it. My name is Father Tarsisius, Abbot of the Monastery."

Propping myself up against the wall, I said I was also very glad to have made it. Behind him I could see a vast blue sky and the sun already shining brightly.

"I have a letter here from Br. David. Why don't you read it and I'll be back in about an hour." He handed me a thick envelope and left the room.

I opened it with care and unfolded what seemed to be several pages. After reading a couple of pages I began to feel ill. The letter said that The Grange was now to be moved to an island in Maine called "Mt. Desert." Here was a bit of divine comedy, as I now sat in my bed in the middle of the wilderness of New Mexico, with the community now at the opposite end of the United States on some island called 'Mt. Desert!' As I read on, Br. David said that he had tried to reach me without success before I left. He then indicated that there might be someone in Espanola with whom I might still catch a ride. Otherwise, he wrote, maybe it was "providence" that I was there.

"Providence...hmm," I thought. I could only think of pilgrims and Providence, Rhode Island. It seemed such a fateful word pointing towards finality. "Providence," felt like giving up and settling for the situation or place. I started to feel panicky.

Was there a reason for missing Br. David's phone calls before embarking on this trip? Was I to be a monk here? Was this the end of line? "No," I thought. "It can't be. Maybe I'm here to simply see this beautiful environment?" I felt confused. I knew that there were only a couple of monks at the monastery, and wondered if perhaps I was needed here.

Looking out my door into this vast country of mesas, mountains and blue sky I found myself trying to make sense of it all. Trying to probe for deeper meaning, I looked around my room. It was simple, not cluttered as if telling me to also keep it simple. I could see the simplicity in the sky and the mesa valley—quiet...serene. For a moment everything seemed to take on a different quality of its' own. I didn't feel alone.

Land of Enchantment

> *A grain of corn contains the Universe:*
> *The hills and rivers fill a small cooking pot.*
>
> Zen Master Huang Lung

Father Tarsisius reappears a couple of hours later.

"Did you read the letter?"

"Yes, I did," nodding my head.

We both looked at each other or, should I say, stared at each other. I wasn't sure what to say next.

"You probably need time to think about this John? I can imagine how you must feel."

"Yes...a bit dazed."

"It will work out. Maybe it is providence that you are here."

For a moment, I began to wonder whether there was some divine intervention at work here.

"Could I ask a favor of you John?"

"Sure," I said, feeling anything but confident. "What is it?"

"The monks and I were planning to spend several days in Santa Fe and we were wondering if you could caretake the monastery while we're gone?"

"Yeah...sure...I would be happy to." Still feeling fuzzy I basically mouth the words.

"Thank you. By the way, there is a Catholic priest here who just recently got out of the psychiatric hospital. He is on retreat here for a month. I would be grateful if you could keep an eye on him. Also, don't worry there is plenty of food in the kitchen."

"Are you and the brothers planning to do anything special while in Santa Fe?"

"Nothing special. It's recreation time for us. We were planning to see the Charles Bronson movie called, "Death Wish." "Interesting," I thought. "I wonder what motivates them to see that and not some "feel good adventure story." I guess we all need a hero story, even if the hero is the one that blows away the bad guys.

Reaching out with both arms to embrace me he turns around and leaves. I stand there in my underwear, but felt even more naked. Was this what it was like to be a *sadhu*—in his loincloth, living in the wilderness, exposed to the elements? With all that had just happened, I wondered if maybe I shouldn't rush out to take my abode where plenty of caves and rocky outcrops stood ready to hide me.

Stepping out of my room I looked out upon the valley and mesas. The blue sky was endless blue upon blue. A lone cloud would occasionally float by as if to pay a visit and look down from above. The layered rocks expose a variety of colors, each telling its own unique tale of time and creation. The slopes and mesas topped with juniper and *pinon* trees.

Seeing all this made me reflect on a discussion I once had with my Zen teacher:

Zen Master: Human beings, materials and so-called mind are one—three is one...one is all. Then here is the origin of all modern thought. For instance, Marxism divided material and mind. But Buddhism, in "Avatamsaka Sutra," saw them as one. Materials and mind are the same thing. You cannot divide it.

John: Expression of how you use your materials is how you use your mind.

ZM: In deep understanding of being, there's understanding of material, idea, as one—same. Even to this day, the scientist divides the organic and inorganic matters. They divide spirit/mind and matter into two fields...sort of. But Buddhists see as one. We can understand the importance of the harmonious emotions between two persons...so called love, respect and trust. And some people can understand the same harmonious emotions between we and trees. The same can be said between animals and we. Also the same harmonious emotions is happening day after day between trees and animals. Sometimes we are not seeing, or forgetting that. Still this harmonious emotion is happening between tree or animal or rocks, soil, water, all these matters.

Therefore what is important for us is to be fully aware of what the world is. We must see all sorts of emotions between things and beings.

John: You're saying then that trees, animals, plants and so forth, all have emotions that extend to each other. Communicating to each other.

ZM: Exactly.

John: Do you think that we human beings have lost our emotional contact with our environment?

ZM: Yes. Someone may describe the beautiful moon, beautiful trees reflecting on the water and we call him a poet. But if you are really a poet, you must be able to understand that relation in every being...between they and them. That is a real poet. The modern poet has forgotten that. Always they dwell between themselves and the other...some sensitive collective creatures. Often it's just another passion.

John: We are just not seeing the world as a whole...complete.

ZM: Yes. In other words, Shakespeare saw the emotion between Romeo and Juliet, but there was also a frog communicating with Romeo and Juliet.

John: A frog?

ZM: Juliet and Romeo were completely ignorant of the relation...cut off. They were too busy for their own matters. Like when a dog approaches you, physically, yet you can ignore it because you are too busy for your own matters. There are a thousand emotions between each other, talking in a sense. Evidently Truth is offering fragrance to us. Rose is offering color and fragrance. Everything is giving to each other...offering...giving messages and we are ignoring all this.

John: Not giving attention to that because we are so wrapped up in ourselves.

ZM: Sometimes we are calling ourselves very thoughtful beings.

John: We sometimes think we are very sensitive.

ZM: So dull we are! (Laughs) So blind! So deaf! Then here is what I'd like to say. Emotion between human beings is certainly important, we agree. Between we and animals, trees and we are important too, we agree. But before that and after that, most important emotion is between materials and material. Their emotion is most important.

John: Materials and materials?

ZM: Emotion between rock and rock.

John: Most important?

ZM: Most important! Lasting before mankind...and lasting after mankind. And...there is a sound between dirt and dirt. There are emotions going on.

John: Because that was the origin.

ZM: That was the origin...so...without understanding that part how can, or could we understand our emotions completely. Impossible...See?

John: I wonder if that's why when I go to the Southwest there's something that I can feel in touch with. The place has a primitive original vitality. This is where life started! To see the desert, the rocks...

ZM: So! Then if we truly can realize communication, or emotion between materials...then we can say, materials and all sort of beings, organic beings and our mind—intelligence, are all intercommunicating. And that's the entrance of understanding that we are not lonely people, not lonely creatures. We are part of them and also at once, some part independent. And even if we were orbited into space, still we are not lonely. We are basically material...one matter, simply.

John: Physical.

ZM: Yes. On that basis we are all common. We share the basic equality of every being. So...we must remind ourselves that stage of understanding.

John: So you think if we could communicate and give our attention to all these things around, the problems we create for each other would be less?

ZM: Much, much less. First of all...no loneliness, therefore no abusing others. That's an original problem of human beings—thinking they are alone, and therefore we like to protect things or possess them by ourselves...distrusting every surrounding being. Therefore, if we understand all common equality between every being, then we can be harmonious. We can be relaxed (stretching out on bamboo chairs, we shared a laugh).

Discussion took place in Kyoto, Japan

All things in nature work silently. They come into being and possess nothing. They fulfill their function and make no claim. All things alike do their work, and then we see them subside. When they have reached their bloom each returns to its origin. Returning to their origin means rest, or fulfillment of destiny. This reversion is an eternal law. To know that law is wisdom.

Tao Te Ching

*The truly awake know all things
Are non-dual, beyond duality, all equal
Inherently pure as space,
Not distinguishing self and non-self.*

Avatamsaka Sutra

We wish to call everything "mine," or "my right to have."

There is no greater offense than harboring desires.
There is no greater disaster than discontent.
There is no greater misfortune than wanting more.
              Tao Te Ching

In this world of limited space, it's very sad to see those who have money buying up property left and right, building on it with neglect. There are those with little who simply have no awareness or care to preserve the environment, much less their own home. I can easily see why the American Indians were deeply saddened by what they saw happening. In their view, we are travelers or visitors on this planet. Nature nourishes us, gives life to us, yet we turn around and are extremely neglectful and abusive towards Her.

Nature is also giving us signs that we need to be careful or we will inevitably destroy ourselves.

The earth is beautiful and the more aware of it you are, the more beautiful it is.

The Grange

While the monks in Santa Fe were watching their Charles Bronson movie, I was agonizing over what to do. On the one hand it did feel like providence had led me here, but on the other it felt as though this was just a momentary delay and that I should continue on to Maine. And yet, I liked it here.

In the several days that followed there was nothing to do but be quiet. Minutes stretched onto hours and the space of the canyon continuously exposing itself leaving nothing for the imagination.

The sky is boundlessly wide, the flight of birds is without end.

Zen Teacher Hungjy Jengjiau

"So what now?" I wondered if they had a cold Coke in the refrigerator and walked over to the kitchen to have a look. There it was in the back. I took it and sat down in a rocker in the cool of the adobe library. The only sound to be heard was the slurping of my coke, punctuated by an occasional belch. Unfortunately no one was there to hear it. I thought it a shame that something spontaneous and funny was being missed; though maybe the spirits of the authors of some of these books heard it. Those earthy American writers like Mark Twain or Thoreau would no doubt have appreciated my belching.

I enjoyed the rocker. It gave me a sense of calm. I had settled in and was appreciating the cool and quiet of my surroundings when suddenly I heard a creak. It was the priest.

"Sorry...I didn't mean to disturb you."

"Oh, that's all right. How are you doing today?"

"Very well, thank you. Umm...can I ask you a question?"

"Sure."

"Well...yesterday after dinner when we were washing the dishes, I noticed how much attention you were giving to them."

"The dishes?"

"Yes...you were so careful in washing them." He had a look on his face as though he was waiting for the answer to the meaning of life.

"Well, since they were someone else dishes, I must have given extra attention."

Shaking his head, "No...it was more than that. It was as if you were completely present with everything. I couldn't help but watch you out of the corner of my eye."

I was beginning to wonder what else he might be watching.

"Well maybe it has to do somewhat with my Zen training. My teacher said that when washing dishes and utensils one should take care of them as if they were one's own eyes."

Pondering, the priest said, "I have heard of Zen and am curious to learn more."

"Well...to be frank, my learning has come primarily by doing or action and not so much reading or academic studies. I can tell you in a nutshell what I have learned so far, but of course there is always practicing."

Excited, "Yes! Please do! We Catholic priests learn much of the scholastic and very little of the practical. We are supposed to be these "do-gooders," and yet it sometimes feels like an empty void.

"O.K. then let me tell you."

1. Presence in even the smallest detail.
2. Courage by trusting a little more your innate ability.
3. Take risks sometimes.

4. See every day as a new day.
5. Do a little more for someone than they have done for you—in whatever way that looks.
6. Don't complain or blame. 'Every day is a fine day' as one Zen master once said.

Here my mind drew a blank. I knew there were a few others, but this is what had come up and maybe this was what he needed to hear. He wrote them down meticulously and held them to his chest as something precious. I knew the feeling. Advice or direction given me by my teacher was like receiving a gem. Although I was not formally a teacher to this priest, I must have represented something that was of great importance and value in his life. I was happy that he was happy.

"See you at dinner tonight?" I nodded in response and continued sipping my coke.

In the days that followed I had several visitors, some wondering if I was the abbot. Some brought gifts, mostly of food. If it was sweets or baked goods, my priest friend and I did not take long finishing them off.

One day, a young couple wandered in saying they were hitchhiking from California. That evening they smoked pot and who knows what else and later that evening the girl came on to me. She was quite attractive and in another situation I might have been interested, but it all felt "messy" and I did not want to partake in the event. Instead, I told them that it would be best if they left and that this was not the place for that. They left abruptly, with the guy saying something indiscernible, and the girl giving me a big hug and kiss.

In those days, I spent a lot of time taking walks and sitting in the chapel. Dusk was the best time, when one could look through the large glass windows of the chapel and see the cliffs turning the color of bright orange. In that quiet solitude of that environment I could truly feel being "touched" by something great.

Not knowing what to do about my future however, I resorted to the I-Ching. It was indicating, or so it appeared, for me to stay. I felt alone and yet not alone. It was a weird feeling to be sure, as though there was a hand guiding all of this. It finally occurred to me to just give in to it. I decided that if the monks came back saying there was a person still leaving from Espanola for Maine then I would go, otherwise I wouldn't.

Several days later the brothers showed up. Fr. Tarsisius mentioned that a woman named Donna would be leaving in the next couple of days for Maine. There were mixed feelings, as I was not particularly anxious to go, but I decided to stick with my decision. For the next couple of days I mostly hung out in the porch looking out at the vista, sipping coffee, reading and journaling. I would say these were the happiest couple of days I had ever had. Leaving that place was painful, like being wrenched away from one of my own organs. Even so, I knew that I would be back one day and that the memory of this place would stay deep within me.

Donna was a jovial young Hispanic woman who had spent her whole life in Espanola. While she was excited about living in a new area and being a part of this monastic community, she was already missing the fact that she might not be eating good New Mexican chili for some time. She made sure to bring enough along. Her younger sister Anna was coming along for the ride. I liked her. Aside from being quite beautiful, she also had a certain wit. She had decided to carry some of her herbal loose-leaf tea with her. On our way out we got pulled over at a speed trap and thought that maybe the policeman would take it for marijuana if he ever saw it—fortunately he did not. Instead he slapped me with a speeding fine.

That day our destination was Interstate 25 towards Denver to pick up Cathy, a woman coming in from San Diego, California. "Like totally" she was Californian.

After picking her up, we headed towards Boulder, Colorado. On the way, Cathy entertained me displaying her webbed toes. In Boulder, we met up with Sandra, your hippie, organic/whole foods type of girl with an interest in Hinduism. Like me, she was also exploring her Christian roots. That night she made a great vegetarian cuisine and afterwards, led us into some Hindu chants. We all seemed to get along.

We decided to spend an extra day in Boulder to do a little hiking. I really loved the surrounding Rocky Mountains and would have liked to stay more, but the next morning we got up early and headed out. Our venture took us towards Minnesota, and then upward towards Canada where from there we traveled east. I had never seen this part of the world. Canada was an amazing wilderness—and cold. I ended up doing most of the driving. Cathy usually sat next to me and would massage my head and shoulders. We were finding ourselves attracted to each other.

Finally we got to the border of Vermont. When the Border Patrol asked me where my home was, I couldn't think straight and told them I really had no "real" home since I'd traveled all my life. The word home is difficult to pinpoint...I could say I was from Ohio, but then that wouldn't be quite correct either....

"All right! Step out of the car and all of you take a seat inside the building please!"

I felt like an idiot and Cathy was still massaging my head. About forty minutes later they give us the go ahead. "Thank God!" I thought the tea leaves would definitely look suspicious.

We arrive in Mt. Desert Island... Arcadia National Park...Bar Harbor or "Baa Haabar" in the local lingo—a beautiful place mixed with sea, mountain and marsh. It could also be as cold as shit. It was September, and all of us sat in front of the fireplace. Along with Br. David, Paul and Frank, who were both around my age, had arrived. Paul was a social worker from New York City and a long time friend of Br. David's, and Frank worked for the forestry department. For Frank, whose background was traditional church attendance, this whole venture was completely new. Paul, on the other hand, was also a practitioner of Zen and aware of various spiritual traditions and viewpoints.

Br. David described how he saw people as fitting into the category of either a cat or a dog. Sometimes people could be a cat-like dog or a dog-like cat. When I asked what he thought of me, he said I was not a domestic house cat – but a leopard or jaguar. I took it as a compliment.

We followed a kind of monastic schedule similar to the Benedictines. Our daily life was one of work, study and prayer or meditation. Paul and I got up earlier to sit Zen meditation for about 40 minutes each day. Frank joined us for a little while but then gave it up. Gradually he became more and more withdrawn and finally bolted from the Grange. Meanwhile Cathy and I were getting closer.

We also spent time getting acquainted with the area and taking short trips around the island. Our community plan was to eat only vegetarian, though I think Br. David would have been happy just eating potatoes. As we got into the winter months, the vegetarian meal deal was not going well with me—especially since I was doing a lot of outside work. Though eating massive quantities, I was gradually getting thinner and thinner. Between meals, I would scoop out large spoonfuls of peanut butter to allay my hunger and give me some energy.

Once, when Paul and I were staying at the hermitage down the road, we decided to sneak out and go to a seafood restaurant. The women in the community had been diagnosed with intestinal worms and Paul had heard that eating fish could help prevent it. I, for my part, was craving meat and protein, worms or no worms. So off we went to Bangor and pulled into the first seafood restaurant that we saw. I ordered the "Admiral's Platter," the biggest one you could get, leaving not a scrap at the end of the meal. It felt like a shot in the arm and, when I got back to the hermitage, I made a choice then and there to never go just vegetarian again.

Meat and sex...after a few months, I knew I could not do without these two things. My chances of becoming a full time monk were beginning to look slimmer.

A female German Zen Priest came to visit. She was a student of Sasaki Roshi, a traditional Rinzai Zen teacher who lived mostly in California. I liked her presence. She

The Grange

exuded a kind of Zen-like quality. It was refreshing to have her there for these two weeks since she helped bring people "out" a bit. Donna and Sandra were becoming more hermit-like, or should I say they did what high school teens would do when they are not happy—they isolated. Br. David isolated himself as well and then went on his lecture tour. Cathy and I would have our occasional little arguments about stupid things. Br. David and I also had our disagreements. My leopard side was beginning to come out. More and more it was just like being in a dysfunctional family.

Fortunately there were outings, which helped to lighten up the situation. One day we were taken to a place called Long Island off the coast of Maine. The family we visited who were friends of Br. David seemed a little bit odd. Their cabin was full of teddy bears. It was like entering the twilight zone and not my idea of an enlightening visit. "Sad people," I thought. .

After hiking the small island, we headed back. With a small boat, I rowed us back to the fishing boat, while seals danced and swam around us. Meanwhile, Dan the Fisherman was anxious. A storm was brewing above us. He started the engine and began to head back—a two and a half-hour trip. After about an hour, the sea began to churn...getting worse...until everyone had to get below. Paul had burned his hand while holding on to the hot steam pipe. Sandra tried nursing it with some ice cubes.

Meanwhile, a whole barrel of fish overturned and I tried scooping them back in. It was now pitch-black and all I could see were the stars above. Large troughs of water were taking the boat in every which way. I was hanging on to the side railing and at one point half of my arm was submerged. This was getting serious!

Eventually I was able to make my way over to Dan who, with his focus straight ahead, had an expression of strong intent. He looked at me and shouted ... "We'll make it by God! Maybe this is a good time for prayers or something?" I had already begun.

The small fishing boat was now being thrown in all directions by large, dark and ominous waves making me feel— as though I had entered a black hole. But then all of a sudden I felt a wave of calm engulf me. There was no worry or anxiety and I was amazingly present. Maybe I had just completely accepted the situation.

    Soon after, I began to see lights ahead. Notifying the others, they all breathed a big sigh of relief. The closer we got, the calmer the waves got. Slowly we pulled into port. There were some people, including Dan's wife and some fishermen, who had come out feeling concerned about our predicament, and I was struck by the concern and care everyone had. All of us had the feeling that the hand of God had something to do with our safe passage.

    After about six months at the Grange, it was time for me to go. I talked to Br. David and he said it was fine for me to leave. There was a cabin in the Catskills where Paul said I could live for a while and I decided to go there. It sounded like just the thing. It was located way back in the mountains where, if I chose, I could live in silent retreat and just do my own thing. I started to get back into Sumi painting and calligraphy. I started corresponding with Zenji again. He was at the time quite busy building a temple just outside of Kyoto, Japan. His letters were short, mostly encouraging me to live with courage, kindness and honesty. Whatever I received was very valuable to me.

    For the most part I was enjoying the "back to nature" life, taking my "scream baths" under the cold mountain stream that also served for drinking water. Life was simple and silent in the mountains. Activities were kept to a minimum. Boredom was a challenge at times though, and I found myself missing companionship. One day I decided to hitch hike the twelve miles or so into Woodstock where I heard blues singer and guitarist Muddy Waters, drank beer, had a nice dinner, met some people and then got a ride back to the cabin. That was all I needed for a while.

    I loved to take walks, to look closely at and to sit in nature, to observe the color of the leaves, the sky and the passing clouds, to touch the ground, the rocks and the trees. There was so much in my environment with which to be acquainted. I remember how my teacher used to stroll along and stop at a certain place, such as a tree or a telephone pole and touch it, look at it, press it with his foot, rub the side of it, sometimes making unintelligible sounds. I sensed that he was intimately communicating with these places and things.

There is so much more in this life than our connection to people in this world or to man-made objects. Society is artificial. The natural world is not.

> To know the plum blossoms,
> One's heart,
> One's nose!
> (Haiku poet) Onitsura

An unusual phenomenon happened while I was at the cabin. It was about nine in the evening and a big lightening storm came up out of nowhere. I could hear the lightening crashing all around me, and then at one point there was a loud boom that struck a house down in the valley in a bad way, injuring a couple of people and causing the house to burn down to nothing.

There were numerous lightening streaks across the living room floor about an inch or so off the ground barely missing me. With the electricity knocked out, I sat there quietly in the dark, anxiously watching this strange occurrence of nature. For about five minutes, bright streaks of light shot past missing me by inches, but amazingly I was not hit.

Close Encounters in Alabama

Years later I would find myself wanting to head back to New Mexico. I was living then in Washington DC and working as a graphic artist. My last design and production project was for Christ in the Desert Monastery. In exchange for the design work, I would be allowed to spend several months on retreat deep in the canyon. Though I liked D.C., it was time to move away from the multitudes, traffic and "hum" of politics. Also I was leaving the graphic design business. Mostly computers were doing graphics now, and I had no interest in learning it.

Another reason was that, while in Japan a year earlier visiting my Zen teacher, I read a thousand page manuscript my Zen teacher wrote about his life and training as a monk. With an idea of raising funds for it to get published and an urging on his part, I thought it a worthwhile mission at the time, and I certainly wanted to prove myself as a worthy Zen student.

The car packed to the hilt with my belongings, I decided to travel via Jacksonville, Florida to visit my mother and see the ocean before making my way west. After a few weeks in Jacksonville Beach, I headed out stopping off to visit my Aunt Lou in Quincy, Florida. Then it was on to my grandparent's farm in Cottonwood, Alabama.

It was good to see the farm again as I stood in one of the fields watching the sunset. My grandparents had died about twenty years earlier, but the farm was still being worked. My memories of being on that farm were ones of love and nurturing. One of my favorite pastimes was to rock out on the porch while looking out at the night sky, but nothing was to prepare me for one of the most unusual events that happened one night when my grandfather spotted an oval-shaped silver disk in the sky. I was in the living room watching wrestling out of Dothan, Alabama on the TV, when my grandmother called me in her usual manner "Woo John! Come out here!"

"What it is grandmother?"

"Come out here and take a look in the sky."

I got up from my usual slouched position and slowly walked out to the porch.

"What is that?" my grandmother asked.

Looking up, sure enough to my amazement there was a flying saucer! It was an oval shape, silver and green. I could not believe what I was seeing. It felt as though at that moment I had been instantly transported to another dimension. My grandparents were "simple folk," so I chose not to mention flying saucers or UFO's. Instead I said, "I don't know."

"Get the shot gun!" my grandfather called out.

Running to the kitchen, I grabbed the single barrel shotgun leaning in the corner and loaded it. I ran hurriedly back to the porch where my grandparents sat transfixed on the object. Meanwhile I stood there quietly not moving, not saying a word. Then all of a sudden the UFO dropped from the sky, giant light bulbs covering it, lighting up everything around it in a dazzling white light. The sound seemed a little like a helicopter, but different. All the trees started swishing back and forth as though being blown by a strong hurricane. It hovered in one place for a little while, then moved over to another area and hovered there for a while. Then in another unusual occurrence, the UFO split into two parts. One part came towards the porch. During this whole episode we did not say a thing. We were paralyzed into dead silence.

As the black metallic craft approached, I began to feel apprehensive. It hovered in front of us and after what I would guess to be a couple of minutes; colored rays of light came streaming out of it towards the ground—red, green, blue and yellow. It appeared the rays had no fixed direction, but continued to move about randomly on the ground as if trying to find its mark. At one point the rays moved closer towards us. I remember a yellow ray lighting up the azalea bushes about five feet front of me as I pushed my body back in the chair as far as it could go, hoping the light wouldn't hit me.

The next thing I remember is that the one half of the UFO near us floated back towards the other near the creek and they both converged. It then floated up slightly, moved northward away from us over the distant hill until it disappeared out of sight.

We sat there saying nothing, not even a "Wow...did you see that!" The whole thing seemed to have lasted about twenty minutes, but then why did all three of us suddenly feel tired, especially since then it would have only been around nine-thirty. It's possible it could have been much later. Nonetheless, not a word was mentioned that evening. Quietly I went to my bedroom, got under the covers and stared out the window into the dark night until I fell asleep.

The next day my parents arrived from Mobile, Alabama where they were attending a golden anniversary for my stepfather's parents. My mother enthusiastically asked how our past several days had gone. Grandmother responded saying, "Oh fine.... Oh... (As if remembering something) We did see some strange object in the sky with lots of lights on it."

"What?" my mother asked. "What do you think it was? Did you report it?"

"No..." said my grandmother. "Didn't really think of that. I guess we should have. ...Anyway...How was your trip to Mobile?"

That was pretty much the end of the conversation as I remember. Nothing was ever said of it again.

On A Mission from Buddha

Before leaving Alabama, I wanted to see my Uncle Edwin and Aunt Merle who lived several miles down the road. I got there just in time for a supper of freshly made dishes and leftovers. Eating at Edwin and Merle's house was like being at a small buffet. There would be five courses or more, usually in little bowls or on small plates: Fried chicken, yellow squash, fried okra, rice/gravy, leftover sausage and field peas, and for dessert, moonpie. There was always enough.

This would be my last visit, as Uncle Edwin was to die only a few months later. Aunt Merle died not too long after that. As we hugged our good-byes that day, he stuffed a five-dollar bill in my pocket.

Heading west on Interstate 10, I felt a strange mixture of happiness, sadness and longing—longing for what, I don't know. Pine tree after pine tree flew past me. Soon the terrain was to change.

I headed into Houston, Texas where I stopped off for the night to meet a person who might be interested in helping to finance the book. We met for dinner that evening and he chatted on about Buddhism and his interest in meditation. I could barely get a word in edgewise. The next morning we met again for breakfast. He handed me a clipping of a short story and twenty dollars. I felt deflated and disappointed. Still, I thanked him politely and went on my way.

The story was about a Zen devotee in Japan name Tetsugen who decided to publish the sutras, which at the time were only available in Chinese. The books were to be printed with wood blocks in an edition of seven thousand copies, a huge undertaking.

Tetsugen began traveling and collecting donations for this purpose. Sympathizers would give him gold coins but others would give him only small coins. It happened that at one time the Uji River overflowed, leaving most people in a state of famine. Tetsugen ended up using the money to help, thereby having to start all over again to collect donations. Again another epidemic spread over the country. Again he used up his money. For third time he started collecting donations, and after twenty years his wish was finally fulfilled.

Nice story, but obviously this was not going well. I was, though, comforted by the thought of having raised $1,500 from the sale of artwork from my house in Arlington, Virginia prior to leaving, with the help of a girl friend and a couple of good sized donations. The proceeds were sitting in a money market account at least collecting some interest. It was making more than I was.

Wide open spaces. I love wide-open spaces! Seeing for miles and miles without anything blocking one's view frees the mind and opens the heart. Now I'm in the western portion of Texas angling my way towards New Mexico. The sparsely clouded blue sky stretches on and on into the horizon. Wide open plains with mountains in the distance. The occasional tumbleweed crosses the road, some almost as big as my Honda. Blown by the wind they hit my car, obliterating into dust. Form bursting into formlessness.

Taos, New Mexico bound, land of the mesas and mountains—God's country. Town of the Navaho's, hippies, tourists, movie stars, spiritual seekers, single women trying to find themselves, single men trying to Be themselves, addicts in recovery, Ram Dass leftovers, lovers of nature, ski addicts, and artists of different sorts. Each tries to find their niche in reality under the wide-open azure sky. These are the types of people I would meet while there.

Here enters a Zen student trying to raise funds for a book that no one will ever see until it is published. Nonetheless, I travel and walk the countryside meeting people and trying to have the confidence of someone with an important assignment. My Zen teacher says to "Help the book and the book will help you." Sounds like a nice concept, but I am not so self-assured

In Taos, I stay with a retired person, a friend of a friend in Maryland who had donated towards the book. She was from New York City and still had that New York sharpness to her, but at the same time attempting to be Hindu? Interesting combination and somewhat phony, I thought. In her house chanting and singing with others was an almost daily occurrence. I spent a lot of time in my head figuring out how to approach her for a financial contribution.

A few days later my friend from Maryland flew in and stayed in a local motel with an inside heated pool. Some of my days were spent wrapped in the warmth of the pool while looking out at the snow-capped mountains. One evening after dinner my friend approached our hostess to help me out. She gave the usual response I would hear from others, which is, "How can I contribute to a book I've not seen or really know what it is about?" In my travels, I would attempt to explain this thousand-page book in a nutshell, carrying a few printed excerpts from the book, but it was a waste of time and paper.

"How come your teacher isn't with you doing this or out doing it himself?" Some people ask. My response was usually that, as his student, I was out raising funds, plain and simple. Or I tried to side step the question.

The old lady wouldn't budge and I left empty-handed. I called an ex-girlfriend in Florida. She told me that she couldn't see me as a "Zen salesman." At that point, I couldn't have agreed more.

Winter was in the air as I made my way towards Santa Fe. I had no idea exactly where I was going to stay. Needing to conserve money, I avoided motels. My first stop in Santa Fe was the Albertson's grocery store. I called a female Buddhist priest that I had communicated with by letter before coming. She was abrupt over the phone and said there was nothing she could do, and that besides, it was "strange that I got stuck raising funds without his assistance." A feeling of idiocy and loneliness came over me and I looked up at the Sangre de Cristo Mountains as if to get some comfort. Nothing came back, only the deep-forested green of the landscape.

I entered the store with pangs of hunger. Going down the aisles gazing at the different food products, I wasn't sure what to get. There was a woman in one of the aisles and we struck up a conversation. She was English and had moved to Santa Fe trying to find a different way of life. I told her that I had just rolled into town and was unfamiliar with it. She decided to give me a little walking tour. As we walked out of the store (I didn't get anything) she said how interesting it was that she felt a sense of trust being with me. I nodded. She talked non-stop as we strolled up Guadalupe Street towards San Francisco Street. She introduced me to some of her coworkers at the store—friendly. We strolled up towards the plaza, got a coffee and ice cream and sat in the park.

"OK", she said, "Enough about me. How about you?"

"Oh great..."I thought, "What do I say? Well you see, it all began one stormy evening and...."

"I'm helping to get a book published having to do with Buddhism." There you go John. Good...keep it simple.

"Oh that's interesting. Any luck?"

"A little. Hopefully things will get better."

She didn't appear to want to know more, so I didn't say more. Frankly, I was glad not to have to continue. At that moment, it was not firing my passion. I felt much more related to her soft black hair and clear white skin.

She looked into my eyes and smiled. I smiled back. Since it was getting a little chilly, she suggested that we go to the St. Francis hotel, order a drink and sit in the lobby next to the fireplace. We both ordered margaritas on the rocks and sat looking out at the mountains. She began to tell me how the landscape of New Mexico either pulled you in to protect you and keep you around or else spat you out. I asked her when one would know. She told me to give it six months. At that moment I felt pulled in and accepted, but for how long? All I was sure of was that the margaritas tasted good and potent. I leaned slightly against her as she did me. We watched people come and go in the lobby entrance.

"If you watch long enough you might see a movie star walk in."

"Really?" I asked. "I have a friend back in Washington DC who told me that Cher spent time here."

"Oh yes...her and a number of others. But I hope it doesn't get over-ridden with them. Already there is beginning to be a great division between the rich and poor here. The creative types who have made Santa Fe interesting, other than the rich history it already has, are feeling the money pinch. The more wealth comes in, the more difficult it makes it for others to survive here."

"By the way, are you hungry?"

"Yes...definitely." I responded.

"Why don't we go back to my place and I'll cook a Mexican dish." Off we went to her small adobe cottage. Her kitchen was about the size of a bathroom, but I offered to help. She politely replied "no," so I decided to just sit and observe her prepare the meal.

"Are you married...in a relationship?" she asked.

"No...are you?"

"No" she quickly replied. She stood there cutting a few more vegetables, and then she put down the knife and walking over to me sat on my lap and gave me a long French kiss. She had beautiful full lips and I was not about to part my lips from them. After a few minutes she stood up and walked back over to the kitchen, about three feet away.

"I'm very attracted to you, but I'm just not going to go to bed with you," she said.

I had not thought about sleeping with her, but I was hoping to crash at her place even if on the sofa or floor.

"No I won't do it, unless you can make a commitment to me."

"A commitment? I barely know you." It felt so abrupt; I wasn't quite sure what to think.

"We can learn more about each other, but before I have you stay I need your confirmation." I could easily have answered "Yes..." stay...have good sex, and then leave promising to see her again soon. But somehow I didn't feel right about someone very intent on having a relationship with me. At the same time I had no idea what would happen next with me.

"I just can't make that kind of commitment." I said. "But I would like to see you again at some point." She appeared a little sad and frustrated. Quietly with a few nice words spoken we ate our meal. The tone seems to have changed so quickly and I was still trying to make out how in just one day of meeting, that she would want to make some kind of commitment. I was saddened as well.

When we finish she said, "Well, maybe I'll see you again, but I know that I won't have you stay the night here tonight." Politely thanking her, I gave her a big hug and walked out towards my car. It was just starting to snow and the air was thin and cold. She stood in the doorway of her house and watched me get into my car. The landscape didn't spit me out, but rather a woman desperate for companionship. I looked up at the pitch-black night and bright stars.

Now what? As I made my way down the highway towards Espanola, I looked for possible places to stop and spend the night. It was about one in the morning and I was feeling quite tired and a little drained. The snow continued to fall and it was getting colder. At last I found an entrance to a RV park. No one seemed to be up and around, so I pulled in and found an opening next to a picnic table. My car was packed full of my earthly belongings. Leaning my seat back and pulling out my sleeping bag to cover me, I felt snug and warm enough.

Drifting off, I thought of what it would have been like with her, but then quickly dismissed the thought; though I would have liked being next to a warm female body, with no strings attached. "I wonder how my cat Ms. Kitty's doing at her new home...?" Finally I fell asleep.

The next morning I woke up early. The sky was clear and beyond the mesas the sun has not quite shown itself. Light snow scattered the ground. Turning on the engine I drive quietly out and head onwards towards Abiquiu, destination...Christ in the Desert Monastery.

Down into the Canyon

This did not appear to be the day that I would make it down into the canyon. As I stood on that dirt road with mud all around my feet, I knew I would not get to the monastery. "If I had a four-wheeler," I thought, "I might be able to do it, but not in my little Honda...no way." Instead I sat in my car and ate some food and looked out at one of the mesas. It was huge, jutting out from the flat plains. The air was so clear, I felt as though I was sitting right next to it, although it must have been at least a few miles away.

Sitting there, time passed as though it was never there. The sky was darkening and I could see clouds coming in from Colorado in the north. Turning on the walkie-talkie, I tuned in to the weather channel. More snow coming. "Great..." I thought, "now I'm not sure when I'll get down there." The winds were picking up...stronger and stronger they got, and then a few flurries of snow. The repeated message was "snow coming, snow coming." Although I knew that there was no way I'd get down the canyon, I kept sitting there. After briefly entertaining the idea of camping, I opted for the vision of a good hot shower and some stupid show on TV. So turning around, I headed towards the town of Espanola to find a cheap motel.

The motel in Espanola was a bit of a dump, but at least it kept me from the cold. It did have a television and I watched some old western film. Very fitting. That night I slept soundly with thoughts of the open sky and rugged wilderness.

"OK, now I'm ready!" The sky had cleared the next morning and I was psyched about getting to the canyon again and starting the journey down. My first stop was Joanna's restaurant. Joanna was a very kind middle-aged Hispanic woman who would go around to everyone's table to see if they were all right and that their food was okay. Mine couldn't have been better. The red and green chili was fresh and truly hit the spot. But my favorite was the *soppapilla*, a type of fried flat bread that was served up warm with honey on the side. I couldn't get enough of them, so she kept bringing me more.

After the meal, I "rolled" out to the car, thinking that at least if I got stuck in the canyon, I could probably survive for several days with all the *soppapilla* and chili I had just eaten.

Making my way to the edge of the dirt road where it begins to head toward the canyon, I noticed that it was still quite muddy and slippery. Especially slippery! I had never encountered a muddy road that was like ice. This was obviously something unique to this area. The mere attempt to walk it made me slip and slide all over the place. Thinking it would dry up after a few hours, I waited. During my wait I chanted the Lotus Sutra. After an hour there was not much change, so I thought that maybe I should go over to the Ghost Ranch natural museum up the way to see if a ranger from the national forestry was going to be heading down. There, I met Rodriquez who said that while he might, it was doubtful since the road was even more treacherous the farther one got. It didn't look good. I thanked him and left.

There I stood looking at a long stretch of mud. Slowly I attempted to move up the incline, but my car immediately started to slide back...and then left...right...and semi-circles. I was lucky just to get it back to the paved portion of the road.

I was left standing at the same spot I had started from. It was around one thirty p.m., "Well"...I said to myself, "its make or break time." I grabbed my knapsack and headed down the side of road that I thought might be less slippery. It was, but only by very little, and only because there was an occasional bush to grab on to just in case you were about to fall.

It was very slow going. In ten minutes I must have gone only about a hundred meters, which isn't much, considering I had fourteen miles to go. Yet, I plodded along slowly and methodically. I figured that if I could walk until nightfall, I could camp somewhere along the river and that by morning the road would be better making it possible to get to the monastery that day.

Two hours later I had made it almost two miles and ahead I could see huge mesas and open terrain. It gave me a little hope, but I had really only begun. Walking on, my boots were beginning to feel like cement weights from the accumulation of mud on them slowing down even more my snail-like pace.

Suddenly my thoughts were interrupted by a noise from behind. I stopped and tried to listen. No sound, so I continued along. Thirty seconds later I heard it again. It was hard to figure out what it was, but I guessed that it must be something mechanical. Knowing the condition of the road, I didn't entertain it being a vehicle, but as the sound got nearer it seemed it had to be something like that. I stood there staring in that direction waiting to see what would emerge from over the ridge.

Sure enough it was something mechanical, a vehicle... a Toyota 4-runner, weaving and turning all over the place. It was a sight to behold. I would never have imagined something coming this far without turning back. Whoever was driving this jeep was determined to get where they wanted to go. I could only lean on the staff I was carrying and watch this amusing sight. Eventually it made its way to me.

Stopping, the door flung open and there sat a woman in her late thirties laughing nervously and asking if I needed a lift. I stood there amazed and, playing the part, said, "Let me think about it."

Laughing, "Well..." she said. "When you do, you'll know where to find me." We both laughed.

I can't say why, but there was an immediate attraction. Maybe it was her big blue eyes. She said that she was from San Diego, California and was planning to spend a couple of weeks on retreat at the monastery. She had visited once before and had loved it so much that she wanted to come back. She was married, but I had the impression that it was definitely on the rocks. Her name was Laura.

"Would you do me a favor?" she asked.

"Sure..."

"Could you please do the driving, I don't think I can handle doing this anymore, especially knowing what it is like ahead."

I gave her a nod of assurance and climbed in. Putting it into gear, I pressed the gas pedal and away we went, tail weaving, mud flying and a yell..."Yee Ha!" that might give us that extra edge. Yes...this was it, like one of those Dodge truck commercials.

Amazing. Despite the fact that we were careening all over the place, we were actually making progress. I was feeling more confident and little by little I went faster, until I got a little too confident and ended up going backwards out into the field. Laura was beginning to enjoy the ride.

"You seem to be a pro at this."

"Yeah right!" I sarcastically reply.

A couple of miles down we hit a bend in the road, appropriately called "Devil's Bend." It was like being stuck in hell for eternity. For some reason this devil would not let go and the jeep was continuously being pulled in or turned around. I tried every which way to straighten it out and get it to go on course. It just would not give.

"O.K. Laura...how would you feel if I just risked it and went full blast?" She nodded an affirmation and the twinkle in her blue eyes gave me the impression that she hoped I would say that.

Backing up slowly, I turned the wheel in the direction that I thought would best get us through.

"All right...this is it!" This time she let out a yell and we went surging ahead, mud raining down all over. We went right for the ditch, and just when it seemed like we weren't going to make it, somehow the road flung us around in our needed direction. Giving it more gas, the jeep bucked ahead and ground the earth as if the car itself was not about to give in to the devil. Gaining traction it moved with power down the road until we were clear.

"Man! Was that a trip or what?" Laura put one arm around me and gave me a squeeze. "O.K," I thought to myself, now I know we were to make this journey together.

Laura and I continued slip sliding our way down the road not knowing what to expect next. About a mile down the road we met up with our next "devil." An arroyo or large ditch that was ready to soak up any vehicle headed towards it. Stopping the Toyota I got out and surveyed the area over and over. There were only two choices...one, to make a fast run for it, or two, to call it a night and try early the next morning. I decided on the latter. Even if we made that arroyo we still had about nine more miles to go and across some rugged terrain that would drop about a hundred feet straight into the Chama River. It did not look promising!

"You know John...I have some snacks and drinks in the back. So we would be fine tonight in the way of food."

"Are you a Cub Scout Den Mother? You are prepared!"

"Hardly...I got some of this for the monks, but this is an emergency, wouldn't you say?" --no disagreement from me.

That night we ate, drank and listened to the coyotes howl back and forth to each other. Later, Laura pulled out a photo album and showed me pictures of her pottery and sculptures, and some of her daughter who also lived in San Diego. This was her second trip to Christ in the Desert, but this time she felt freer because of having separated from her husband of 17 years.

"When did you first come here?"

"Back in 1976. I was thinking seriously of being a monk."

"I assume you are not a monk, although you seem to give one an impression that you are."

Curiously I asked her, "how's that."

Looking at me directly with her big blue eyes, "I don't know really, but you seem to have this monkish aura surrounding you."

"Monkish aura!" We both laughed. I again looked at her eyes. She had the largest blue pupils I had ever seen, and felt myself wanting to sink into them.

"What then changed your mind?"

I paused and thought for a while.

"Women!"

"Women?"

"Yes...I knew I wanted to share life with another...of the opposite sex, that is. Being around a bunch of men day in and day out was not my idea of a good time." Again we both laughed.

Laura had one large blanket and we wrapped ourselves in it. It was getting late and we were showing signs of being tired. It wasn't long before we fell asleep in our seats. The coyotes stopped howling, calling it a night too.

On awakening, the first thing I saw was a falling of soft white snow. I got out of the Toyota to check the road. It had frozen and since the sun had not come up, I thought would be a good time to make a dash to the monastery before the road got muddy again.

With Laura still asleep, I started driving quickly down the road. I still had to be careful around some of the bends where there was only a foot clearance from the edge. One miscalculation would translate into "adios amigos!" The more dangerous muddy stretch was in the first five miles, after that the cliffs changed into stretches of open plain. I heard the crunching of frozen dirt from under the tires, and just peering over the mesas the sun threatening to warm the whole place up in a matter of minutes. So far so good and just ahead was the chapel being hit by the sun and radiating a bright orange-like color. Slowly I went through the gates. Laura had awoken somewhat surprised we had made it all the way. Truthfully I was too.

We could hear the bells ringing for the office of lauds (Morning Prayer), so we made our way over hoping to meet the guest master. After Lauds, Brother Leo came up and greeted us warmly and said that our rooms were ready. As fortune would have it, our rooms were next to each other, so in the several days to come there was a lot of...let's say...visitation.

Down into the Canyon

Laura said that she had had a dream the night before meeting me about someone that looked like a female goddess. When she described it, I thought she appeared like Kwan-Yin or Bodhisattva Avalokitesvara the Goddess of Compassion. The previous day before heading out down the monastery road I had chanted the Lotus Sutra, the most important sutra in Buddhism. Was there a correlation?

Avalokitesvara helps sentient beings below while seeking and encouraging the Buddhahood above. There is a place where the spiritual world meets the material or phenomenal world. Both worlds connect and support each other. I had, though frustrated and discouraged at times, donated my life to something I felt to be greater. It isn't about whether one has the ability or not, but whether one is willing to walk or not. This donated life was the Bodhisattva mind itself.

One early evening after I'd settled in, I was sitting in my room writing letters, when I heard a cry coming from one of the mesas. It had an almost human quality to it. The sound was eerie, like someone lamenting over a dead one or the sound of a *shakuhachi* (Japanese flute). There was a painful profundity to its voice as it sailed across the canyon to distant ears.

Soon others joined in with similar voices as if in chorus. They all howled back and forth to each other as the dusk began disappearing. Occasionally the howling would change to yelping or short snapping barks.

The more I listened, the more absorbed I became. I lost all interest in writing. Goose bumps started to shrink and I just sat there listening to them talk and wondering what messages they might be conveying to each other. I put on a sweater and walked out into the courtyard hoping to see one of them, but the sun had pretty much descended and it was difficult to even make out the juniper trees.

Despite these hungry sad voices, there was something wonderfully fulfilling in hearing these coyotes—

48

something that touched me deep inside. Maybe it was their cry that was so familiar. A cry shared by all Beings. In that collective cry we are never truly alone.

      For about a half and hour the yelping continued and then abruptly it stopped. The evening became still and silent...and colder. I walked over to the woodpile and gathered some to put in my room for the evening and then walked over to the kitchen to see if there was anything easy to cook up. For some reason the coyotes had made me very hungry so I cut three slices of whole wheat bread and spread a thick layer of peanut butter—the mainstay of monastic diet.

Balls of Light

After Laura left, we stayed in touch. Almost every day I got a letter and was getting used to it. If a day passed without one, I would get anxious.

Later she flew back into Albuquerque and stayed with a woman she had previously met. When we saw each other we practically flung ourselves at each other like two weeds in the wind. We were both on some kind of love high. It was soon settled that we were going to rent an old adobe house in Abiquiu from her newfound friend, Dorothy, a retired dentist from Houston, Texas who was soaking up the romance vicariously. She too wanted the dream to be true.

The house itself was quite original. Built in the early 1900's, it was made of thick adobe bricks, the kind that would either keep warm or cool for long periods of time. The floors were still dirt except for large Navaho rugs that covered them. Heating was provided by a potbelly stove and there was electricity. Most meals were cooked in the electric wok or toaster oven. The water, mostly composed of iron, was a natural colonic. So farting was sometimes our entertainment, the natural way, during which we would break into fits of laughter.

The house sat in what was called the lowlands, a little back in the canyon but near the main road. The canyon, called Red Canyon went back for miles and miles. This was our backyard...home for coyotes, wolves, owls, cougars, and elk, not to mention witches and bright lights. Across the road was the Chama River and a grape vineyard which desperately needed tending. I took it upon myself to try and get it going again.

Truly, this place was beautiful! –The deep blue color of the sky, the red-oranges of the cliffs, the changing greens of the mesas. It was peaceful and yet dynamic, easy for one to blend in with the rocks and sky.

Laura and I were meanwhile living the high desert life and cash was running low. Still, life was simple, so we didn't need a lot. I had already begun to do photography of the area, so I went to work assembling cards and framed landscape photos to sell in Abiquiu, Santa Fe and Taos. I did quite well and a number of people encouraged me to do a show and/or publish them.

Laura went to work at the Abiquiu Inn, working the front desk and also tried to sell some of her sculptures. For a summer I worked as the weekend cook, learning a variety of dishes: American, Italian, Mexican, and Middle Eastern and some of my own specials of the evening. An American Muslim family, who also became our friends, managed the Abiquiu Inn. Not far from the inn, on top of a mesa, sat a mosque. At one time, as I understood it, Abiquiu had been an important "Mecca" for Islamic people to practice their faith. Apparently later there was some falling out, so it didn't progress as they hoped, leaving the mosque unfinished and several empty adobe houses scattered throughout the property.

"Eeee, Juan! Life is crazy!"

"How's that Maria?" Maria was one of the waitresses at the Abiquiu Inn who usually started a conversation with "Eeee, Juan."

"Last night... I just wanted to wind down, so I got a six-pack of Budweiser and parked my car up at Blue Mesa. So while I'm sitting dere, getting relaxed and all, I start hearing wolves around me howling. I didn't think noting of it at first, but den, eeee...I saw all these lights in front of me. I was sooooo scared!"

"What do you think it was?"

"I don't knooow...eeee...but dere are all kinds of strange tings around here! I guzzled my beer and got the hell out of dere. I need (laughing) to cut down on the beer or something. But I do love my beer."

I knew it wasn't just the alcohol effecting Maria, since it was not long after that I saw what they call balls of light. Some believe they are UFO's, some...atmospheric changes and others believe are brujas (witches) transforming themselves.

My friend Patrick, an actor from New York, came for a visit once. He had never been in this kind of environment, so already it was blowing his mind. That first evening around 9:30, he and I went for a walk in my backyard. It was within five minutes that Patrick noticed a bright ball above our head. When he pointed it out, I said I thought that it was probably a meteorite, but quickly took it back.

It was only fifty meters from the top of our heads sitting there, not moving at all; perfectly round, the size of a basketball and dazzling white. We both stood transfixed.

Within a minute the ball of light began to bob back and forth like a bouncing ball. Then it twirled around in several circles until it spun out about a hundred meters changing different colors, reddish-blue, orange, white and then finally fizzling into nothing.

We thought that might be it, until we saw one further away. Over the cliff was another one that repeated a similar motion. Patrick and I just muttered our surprise at what we saw. We continued walking up one of the hills and sat down to ascertain exactly what we had just seen. As we were talking, I noticed out of the corner of my eye another one over the other cliff. This one was huge; at least three times the size of the others. I told Patrick to turn his head very slowly and try to see it from the corner of his eye. It seemed that if we just looked at it point blank, the light would start to react. Maybe it was just my imagination, but it felt like these balls of light could sense us.

Like the other two, this ball of light also made similar motions, although these were larger sweeping movements. Finally it too fizzled out into the distant night sky leaving us sitting there amazed.

It had all seemed unreal. Patrick and I were dumbfounded and dazed to say the least. I tried to describe it to Laura. She was disappointed not to have seen it, but intuited something profoundly had happened to us.

All Patrick and I could do for the rest of the evening was to shake our heads in disbelieve as Laura served us hot chamomile tea.

The Vineyard

The vineyard across the road was badly in need of repair and I was eager to take on the task. There was an old yellow tractor sitting in the yard that had not been used for some time. I thought I'd see if I could get it going again. The field needed a lot of clearing and I wasn't enthusiastic about doing it all by hand. Not being mechanical by any stretch of the imagination, I was good at analyzing and figuring things out. After fooling with a few wires I was able to jump-start the tractor with my car battery. After about twenty minutes of tinkering...eureka! It kicked over with that loud tractor-like sound that makes one feel like they really mean business! Off I went, tearing across the road to the field. Up and down the lanes of the vineyard I cleared away brush and stones, then swinging around to churn the dirt up, when... all of a sudden the tractor began to lose power and finally, clunk! I tried to start it up, but no go.

Trying to be patient, I walked over got my car and drove it next to the tractor. Hooking the cables up and tinkering a little with the wires, I was able to a get it going again. I quickly drove my car back to the house and then ran back over to the field hoping the engine was still running. It was, so I continued.

The next day the same thing happened. Now I was getting frustrated. It looked like this would take much more time than I had thought and that I might end up doing some work by hand. I did not relish the prospect.

While contemplating the situation, I noticed an older Hispanic man perched on his fence in the next field, watching me with a grin on his face. He was taking the whole thing in. "Instead of standing here like one of these clods of dirt, I should go meet him," I thought. Walking over to him slowly I acted as though I had things under control.

"Trying to get that vineyard going again, huh?" He tilted his cowboy hat a little bit back on his head to get a better look at me.

The Vineyard

"Yeah...that's my objective."

Again a big grin came over his face. He looked at me then looked up at the sky. Nothing was said for a few minutes.

Finally, "I've been watching you with the yellow thing." His eyes seemed to penetrate mine. I found it hard to look too long into them, so I averted my eyes off into the distance.

"You mean the tractor?" I assumed that that was what he was talking about, but I was struck by the name he gave it. All of a sudden it became personalized. I laughed.

"Yeah...the yellow thing." I responded. Again there were a few minutes of silence. This time I found myself looking up at the sky with him.

"Don't let the yellow thing get to you. Like everything amigo, even with good intentions...it can get to you soon or a later. Don't ever forget that."

I suddenly felt as though I'd been struck with an electrical current in the back of my neck. Again we stand there quietly looking out beyond the mesas. Then he smiles and excuses himself saying he needed to tend his horses. I shook his hand and told him that I hoped we meet again.

"I'm sure we will amigo...bueno!" Hopping off the fence, he headed towards his pick-up truck. It was getting late so I decided to call it a night and just leave the "yellow thing" in the vineyard field. Taking a deep breath, I head back home.

Tomorrow is another day.

Oh yes...THE BOOK! So what about it? It's not even my book anyhow!

I know my Zen teacher and I conceived the idea of his book being published by raising funds...but now here in New Mexico, my enthusiasm about the project had waned, and my guilt and agony had begun to grow. I continue to meet people here and there, but most of their interest stemmed from mere curiosity. No one ever donated nor gave any other kind of support. The whole thing seemed like a lost cause and a fanciful dream. My image of the wandering Zen monk had come from reading too many of those Zen books. This free spirited person roaming the countryside in search of Truth, only to find that Truth is made up of a daily reality that doesn't necessarily match one's concept.

One elderly woman up in Boulder, Colorado, somewhat well to do and a Trungpa Rinpoche devotee offered shelter in her home and fed me, but that was the extent of it. Mostly it was just to keep her company. Before leaving, she pushed some wads of money in my hand—sixty dollars...enough to get me back to Abiquiu and to treat Laura and me out to Mexican food.

I was starting to feel like I wanted out of it. There was never any response or encouragement from my teacher. Once I talked with him on the phone and he was blunt. He told me to either be completely obedient to him or to find my way and be obedient to that. After that talk, I thought... "O.K. Since he put it that way, I choose the latter!"

It was depressing. I guess I was a failed Zen student.

Here I was though, in the wilderness of New Mexico, not having any real plan about this book anymore. I decide to continue to stay put here in this vast overwhelming beauty.

The sun is so bright and hot now that my brain feels on fire. I have to lie down.

How to walk on this training path is the problem for students. Some do slowly, some do quickly, and some do shallowly or deeply, halfheartedly or whole-heartedly. The differences of how are more various than all the colorful flowers on earth. And they are not important since it is a matter of formality compared to the graveness of whether to walk or not. 'Find each his fitting way' is the only advice, and for the person who is not sure what the fitting way is, 'Go together with companionship.' There is no certain way a person should take, and probably the best way for a person is excellently unique and not best for others.

Seikan Hasegawa

Nothing in this life is sure, and my vineyard was no exception. I tended it every day, and each passer-by offered suggestions or support. I was getting the impression that some of the local folks were happy to see the vineyard being brought back to life. Maybe what keeps some people going is the thought that life doesn't just die, but that all of us are renewed and reborn in some way or the other, just like plants.

"Swoosh!! What the hell is that Laura?"

"I don't know, but it sounds like it's coming from the front yard."

Both of us scrambled to get up to find out what is going on. The sound got louder as I went outside. I couldn't see anything, but the sound was familiar. Soon I found out why. It was the water rushing through the *acequias* (canals). That day was the day they let the water flow out from the Abiquiu reservoir. Laura and I were like two kids in our excitement! We quickly got our coffee and sat by the *acequia*, listening to the sound of the water. To have water in these parts is liked being blessed.

After taking it all in for a while, I got up and started moving the series of gates to get the flow out into the vineyard. Swoosh...it rushed into the field. Laura and I hurriedly got the shovel and hoed grooves in the field angling the water in the right direction. It wasn't long before the water was covering the whole field. I stood there like a proud father who had just given birth. There was something truly satisfying in seeing all my labor come to fruition, even though the grapes still had to grow. I stood there quietly surveying the land with a big smile on my face.

After about twenty minutes a white truck pulled up along side the road. I didn't know who they were, but I figured they were stopping maybe to take a look and compliment me.

"Nice field you got there." A tall Hispanic cowboy with a large black moustache stood there with his, I assumed, assistant or sidekick...a shorter cowboy.

"Thanks...its great to see the water flowing. I think this vineyard is going to do quite well."

"Yup...I bet it will...." Somehow from the tone of his voice, I got the sneaking suspicion that I had done something I shouldn't have.

"Did you get permission to run this water?"

"Permission? No I didn't...was I...?" Neither of them looked at me while the three of us stood there talking to the field. I was beginning to learn that conversation was mostly done in this manner--especially with Native Americans. One could talk for an hour and never look at each other. "Whom do I get in touch with to get permission?"

"The mayor domo." He quickly replied. I had no idea what he was talking about, but went along with it.

"So who is the mayor domo?"

This time he took a quick glance at me, before looking out in the field again. "I am Senor!" I could see the smaller cowboy give a slight chuckle.

I felt this was a stupid question, but I had to ask it anyway, "Can I get permission from you now?"

This time they both chuckled and looked at each other. "Senor...although I am the mayor domo, I am afraid you will have to call my wife and let her know. She'll then put you on a list and at some point will give you a call to tell you what day you can use the water."

All of sudden I felt dread. I thought that I had really blown it and that most likely I wouldn't hear from the mayor domo's wife until I reached the age of sixty. I apologized profusely to him and said it was obviously a grave error on my part. He again glanced at me, gave a

The Vineyard

grin, and left abruptly for his truck with his sidekick following closely behind.

"Mama mia!" I thought to myself. Live and learn. There were obviously rules that I knew nothing about in these parts, and obviously needed to get a little education here. I decided to go talk to Nestor, my neighbor, who had land adjacent to mine and grew alfalfa. He was apologetic that he had not told me about the water situation.

"Yes Juan, you have to be careful and obey the terms here. If not you can get a lot of people mad at you. Only several months ago there was a gunfight over water. Somebody ended up getting hurt."

Now he tells me! At least I had talked to the mayor domo himself otherwise I might have met someone that would not have looked too kindly on what I had done.

Days passed and there was no call and it seemed like things were not looking too good. But then one day, early in the morning, I finally got that call from his wife, telling me to go out right now and use the water. Promptly I jumped up, opened the gates and let the water flow through getting every bit of the field completely wet. It didn't take long, and I felt a sigh of relief that the vineyard finally was getting that needed water.

It wasn't long before there were signs of some growth on the grapevines. Some Benedictine nuns visited me one day offering to weed the field and make sure that all the vines were attached to their wires. As it turned out, we ended up spending the day together, having lunch and going down to Abiquiu Lake. The younger nuns acted just like children, giggling and splashing in the water. I tried to teach two of the nuns how to swim. One got a crush on me, which probably had to do with my holding her body while she learned the motions of swimming...her face turning bright pink as I held her in my arms, breasts almost coming out of her shirt. There was something playfully erotic about the whole thing.

One evening about a week later she showed up at the house to see me. At that time I was in Colorado. Laura said she was quite embarrassed and apologetic not expecting to find her there, but they ended up having a long talk about love, sex and relationships. By the night's end, Sister Mary was thinking seriously about giving up the vocation.

While I was in Boulder, Colorado, the vineyard flourished. But then the birds quickly ate the grapes and a few passers-by on the road helped themselves too. The nuns came out one day and quickly gathered what they could and made jam. Laura had been in San Diego, California visiting her daughter, so didn't get any. So all in all, I reaped nothing, but the enjoyment and experience of it. I did get some jam from the nuns, and it was quite delicious, savoring every little taste of it as though it was my Last Supper.

Two months later Sister Mary left the vocation.

Moving On

Things had become rocky between Laura, and me. I began to feel that maybe things had happened too quickly with us and it was time to end this relationship and to start looking for another place to live.

I wanted to hand the book over to someone else — but who would take on the project? No one would, of course. This was something I had gotten into so I agonized some more. I would take long hikes to try to shrug off the tension and guilt I was feeling but nothing seemed to work. I wished someone would just hand me the money! Sometimes I would think of crazy ideas to get the money, such as going to live in a cave somewhere as an ascetic or sannayasin (holy man). Maybe then some rich old widow from Santa Fe would hear about me and come to offer donations.

This was actually one of my saner ideas considering I was in an area where many were drawn more to the unusual and mystical, than to the usual and conventional. Besides, this sort of thing happens in India. Take the beggar-madman in southern India who was discovered by some rock star while on a pilgrimage. Soon this crazy beggar was set up with his own temple/ashram. I went to see him once while I was in the area and found him to be a happy sort. He constantly smoked *beedis* (Indian cigarettes) and ate snacks or sweets, while one of his female devotees sat close to him looking in amusement seemingly wanting to break out in laughter herself as if it was a cosmic joke.

Anyhow it did not happen and I decided to let the money that I had raised for the book sit in the money market account and accrue interest. "OK...here I am, giving up on the book, my relationship coming to an end, and with no particular direction to go."

One day though as I was looking at "The Reporter," one of the local Santa Fe papers, I noticed there was an open house for people who might be interested in pursuing a career in counseling or art therapy at a place called

Southwestern College. I thought that maybe this was something to explore.

The next week I went and heard their talk, partook in a little psychological experiment and met some of the teachers. I liked what I heard and decided to enroll. I had been interested in psychology since my years in England, when I worked at a halfway house for adults in Hampton Court as part of my independent study for six months. I learned a lot from that experience.

The two giants in the field that captivated me were C.G. Jung and R.D. Laing. I would try to read anything of theirs that I could get my hands on. My literature teacher used to half-jokingly warn the other students, especially the females, I might find out their deepest secrets. Another teacher, a pro-Skinner behaviorist, and I used to engage in frequent discussions and arguments. On one occasion he got so pissed off at me, his face changed to the color of a bright red tomato. I thought he was going to explode any second.

The more I studied psychology, the more my interest in the spiritual realm grew. I began to question deeply the things we call normal. What is normal? If society is normal, then I prefer the abnormal. Already my life overseas and living in the deep south of America taught me how prejudicial and fearful people are. It seemed partly by our fears we determined what is normal. More and more I admired those that stepped out of the norm by questioning it and making the determination to find their own way.

I liked Southwestern College and what it had to offer. As a small private graduate college, one could be more intimate with the course work. The first year combined one's own work on oneself with the academic, and the second year was mostly the academic and practicum. Most students were in their later 30's and upwards which gave them the needed experience to work with other people. There was to a lot of experiential work as well, so different types of media such as art and dance was combined in the study of therapy. I felt strongly that I could benefit from this program rather than the usual university setting.

A couple of years in therapy in Washington, D.C. during a period of anxiety attacks proved to be valuable experience for my time at this school. I found it immensely important to know what one was *actually* feeling and thinking. In my therapy sessions I realized that at times I would assume or think I knew something when I truly didn't. I saw that being really honest with oneself was something one always had to work at.

While Laura was visiting her daughter in San Diego I was taking long walks in my backyard-- a place called "The White Place" or "Plaza Blanca"-- composed of extinct cinder cones and volcanic ash. It was like walking on a Martian landscape. Sometimes the neighboring dogs, dubbed "astro dogs," would join me for the hike.

While at school one day I had lunch with a teacher, Emma, who said she was looking for someone to house sit her place in Santa Fe. I jumped at the opportunity. This was a good time to talk to Laura and tell her that I needed to leave. Although I was going to miss this area greatly, I intuited an urgency to get out as quickly as I could. Intense involvements can sometimes make for intense departures. Packing up a few belongings I headed to Santa Fe.

Emma was a very active woman with fire red hair, always running off to some workshop or seminar. She loved to create her own music through singing and drumming. I once did a photo shoot for one of her music tapes out in Chaco Canyon, an old Anasazi ruin in the northwest part of New Mexico. Fond of undertaking different projects she often wanted to get me involved in various activities or to meet some new person she had just met or heard about.

Once Emma invited me to meet an old curandera (a good witch) who had just come from Mexico. She was the mother of a Toltec shaman that Emma had studied with at one time. Emma felt that maybe the curandera could help with my shoulder pain and recurring stomach discomfort. I was reluctant at first, but felt I had nothing to lose, so I went. The curandera was in her eighties. She looked and dressed like a peasant and didn't speak a word of English, so her grandson helped translate. She began by praying and then, laying me flat on my back, passed an egg over me, and then cracked it into a glass of water to look at it. She saw the stomach problems and also said there were some bad spirits trying to create problems for me. The curandera then proceeded with her fingernail to simulate something like surgery, as she made motions of cutting me open and then sweeping her hand across my body as if to clear or clean something out. This went on for about twenty minutes.

After she finished she told me to get up slowly. I definitely noticed a kind of change as though I had been cut open and was feeling the after effects. I felt my strength wane as I got off the table. I wanted to go do a little exercise but she told me not to do anything for three days. She handed me a cotton ball that she had wiped me with and told me to put it in a glass of water next to my bed. In the middle of the night she would come to get rid of those bad spirits. I did exactly as she said.

On my way out I thought, "Maybe I'll just go swimming, there can't be anyway it would affect me if I just take it slowly." Wrong! After a couple of laps I found myself already tired, feeling like limp spaghetti. I retired to the house and spent the rest of the time primarily on the couch.

The next week I went to have her check me out. This time she held my hands for a long time and prayed in Spanish. Her grandson tried to keep up with the translation. Then after about five minutes, her hands started shaking. She continued to shake even more. I looked at the grandson trying to figure out what was going on. He wasn't sure and so asked. The curandera was in a type of trance. Finally she was able to say something.

"She's wanting to know if you ever encountered UFOs." I was very surprised at the question.

"Yes I have. A couple of times in fact." I went on to tell her that once in was in Alabama and then another time just recently in New Mexico.

"I thought so," she replied.

"What does this mean?" I was curious what it had to do with my health.

"It is about your spirit guide," she responded. "It is very rare to have a client like you. "In all the time in working with people, I have only met three." At this point I was not sure what to believe. It seemed to me farfetched, but looking at her she seemed quite sincere about it. "I would like you to come back in a few days. I need to find your spirit guide so you will from now on know. This guide will be important for you."

Giving me a hug and then saying another prayer while clutching my hands, we got up together and went into the living room. She immediately told her son that I was an advanced spiritual person. He told her that he could see that when I had first come. Before leaving she gave me a hug and a kiss on the cheek. I walked out to my car not knowing what to think.

It was in the morning and the curandera appeared in good spirits. Taking my hand she led me into another room of the house that I had not been before. This time she sat facing me smiling, and pulling out a piece of paper. It was the name of my spirit guide who was from another planet but had come here to help me along. I was told by her not to ever reveal this name to anyone. This was for only me to know.

That was that except for some herbs I was told she would be sending me to help my stomach and clear out anything that might be remaining. In about two weeks I received them and they ended up lasting me a month. Amazingly it did clear up any stomach problems and gave a boost to my energy. In the days that followed, I could not help thinking fondly of her and how grateful I was.

After several months of living at Emma's house it was time for me to move out and get my own place. Through a classmate of mine, I heard of a place about 30 miles outside of Santa Fe called Chimayo.

Chimayo is nestled in a valley in the Sangre de Cristo Mountains and its culture has been around for hundreds of years. Spanish colonists settled the area in the late 1600's. They were mainly farmers and artisans whose occupations included weaving and stock raising. Weaving is still important in Chimayo and the area is known for high-quality woven goods.

Around 1810, a Chimayo friar was performing penances when he saw a light bursting from a hillside. Digging, he found a crucifix. A local priest brought the crucifix to Santa Cruz, but three times it disappeared and was later found back in its hole. By the third time, everyone understood that it was meant to remain on the site, and so a chapel, the Sanctuario, was built. The crucifix that began the original shrine still resides on the chapel altar. Each year at Easter thousands of people make a pilgrimage to Chimayo to visit the Sanctuario and El Posito, the "sacred sand pit" where the crucifix was found and to take away a bit of sacred dirt.

My house was nothing special, though it had a big yard with some farmland around it and one could see Truchas Peak in the distance. My neighbors were all Hispanic. Some had been there for several generations-- all very friendly, invited me to their homes to eat or to come to a local festival. I was beginning to feel more a part of a family rather than some Anglo living my separate existence. Actually this was the first time that I had felt a part of a community. I liked the idea of not living in Santa Fe because of this.

Cash was beginning to diminish again, so I needed to get some work. I was getting into the mental health field and someone at school mentioned a psychiatric hospital in the area. So, I applied and worked as a mental health technician and later, after gaining more experience, as a counselor. At first I worked with adolescents and later with adults. The adolescents had mostly behavioral problems from neglect or rejection. With adults there was a deepening of behavioral problems and an inability or confusion to clearly understand his or her place in life. For adolescents it was building a healthy self, while for adults it was the meaning of self.

In all, as I suspected in my late teens and as I saw again by working at the hospital, the world itself was unhealthy, yet paraded itself as a stand-in for a healthy existence. The status quo was the image or idea that all of us had bought into without really questioning it. We were being alienating to the point of cruelty without really knowing it.

While working there, I was to meet a person who would have an impact on my life.

Mary

*Mind is the root of bondage and liberation
Of good and evil,
Of sin and holiness.*

Nityananda

I met Mary while studying counseling and psychotherapy and working at Juniper Hills Hospital in Albuquerque. After about a year and a half there, I was called in one day to the hospital to work primarily with a certain woman named Mary who had been admitted two nights before with a diagnosis of multiple personality disorder.

Mary was a medium sized woman about five-foot eight inches tall and in her early forties. I could tell right off the bat from the way she spoke, that she was an intelligent woman. Mary was shy, but I found her to be warm and friendly, and it wasn't too long before she opened up. She came from a fairly well to do family. She was married, though separated, with a couple of children.

Three to four times a week I would go to the hospital and during those days Mary and I and would spend some time together. After a couple of months, she was released to a residential treatment center just outside of town, where they predominately worked with multiple personalities or Dissociative Disorders, with a primary focus on ritual abuse. Mesa Healing Center was set up, not like a psychiatric hospital, but more like a communal living center, where each resident shared in cooking and cleaning. One would live in either an adobe house or a small log cabin.

Mary told me that somehow I had a real knack for working with multiple personalities. She had gone through different therapists; different staff and they had just not connected with her. She said that I had made this connection. I didn't think much about this at the time, other than to thank her for her observation.

Two months later, a woman with a rather gruff sounding voice called. She said, "I'm Kathy, the on-site counselor, here at a the Mesa Healing Center. We are a treatment center that specializes in MPD's. Mary has been transferred here and has told me about you. She couldn't stop saying good things about you. She told me how at the hospital you were able to understand and really help her. I've never heard her say this about anyone else. After hearing this and about what you had done and how you were able to connect with her, I was wondering if you would be interested in an interview and in possibly doing work over here." I said, "Sure, we could get together." She said, "Well, I'm going to talk to the director, Judy, and tell her I'm going to set up an interview."

We met at the Kiva Cafe in Albuquerque and talked. Kathy seemed more interested in my character rather than any specific skills or academic background. They called me back two days later and offered me a position on their staff. So, I went and saw the place and met Judy and gradually lessened my time at the psychiatric hospital. I began working over at Mesa, predominately with Mary.

It was difficult, unusual and interesting work. At the same time it was very draining and would in no time sap my energy if I was not careful. There were many times when Mary would dissociate and I would have to pull her back from going "Elsewhere." It was definitely on-the-job training. There was not much out there in the way of MPD and ritual abuse. So study material was slim.

Ritualized abuse involved alleged situations, as in the case of Mary, where a group of people, following their own religious or satanic ideals, would get together at a particular place in nature, and set up an altar of their making. Here they would then take a young child, predominately a girl, and perform ceremonial rites. Certain people would be entitled to have sex with her. Sometimes she would be left there tied to the altar or tree in the middle of the night.

It's hard to know for certain whether it's true or not, and if so, how much. All I knew was that something traumatic happened to this person that made them "break;" psychologically, emotionally and spiritually. Mary recalled starting to show dissociative symptoms in her later twenties. In my work, I had to be very careful not to put a suggestion or idea in someone's mind, or even allude to something. There were articles coming out at the time about the false memory syndrome, so one had to be very careful about that.

What was beginning to happen with Mary was that she began to later manifest personalities, also known as "alters," and also what we called "fragments" or brainwashing devices that were implanted by the cult "doctor" of the group. The so-called "doctor's" sole purpose in creating these fragments was to protect against any intrusion from outsiders. This was because, as I understood it, they (the group) might be found out and/or also that someone else might alter the victims thinking. All this was carefully planned. In the case of Mary, she had several of these fragments, and to put it bluntly, they were nasty and vicious.

Sometimes a personality would take a nasty turn or "switch" to the bad side. Switching is a term used primarily when the core person changes personalities. One skill I did develop while working there was watching the person's eyes. Through the eyes I could see ahead of time any changes about to occur. Depending on the situation, sometimes I would immediately intercede. With Mary I did a lot of interceding. There were a number of times I had to tell people to leave the room, if something major was about to happen. Mary and I would be left with each other in which sometimes there was a verbal, as well as physical struggle. Eventually I always won out.

One of her personalities was a person named Stanley. Stanley, was originally a "helping" alter, in other words an alter that wasn't going to do bad things to Mary herself, nor to others. On one occasion though, Stanley had gone bad and was dangerous and out of control. It finally took eleven people to contain her at the hospital. This was two days before I first met Mary.

There also was a fragment she called "the Shadow." "The Shadow" was one of the brainwashing devices used as a defense mechanism against anyone "infiltrating" her internal system. When "the Shadow" was beginning to emerge, Mary had been showing signs of improvement, so it came more obvious that the nastier these fragments got, the nearer to the truth we were getting.

When it began to manifest, Mary would see it out of the corner of her eye as blackness. Mostly she believed it was creeping around the outside of her house. Many times she would ask if I saw it. Of course I would reassure her that there wasn't anything there, even after, at times, looking around the house myself. Sometimes Mary would wake up in the middle of the night scared to death, crying and screaming. It was only until we focused on the "Shadow" in one of our therapy sessions that we were able to get rid of it. After that Mary was at a lot more ease.

Once a week I would stay overnight at Mesa as on-site therapist, not just for Mary but for the other residents. Mary would sometimes show up at my cottage at one or two in the morning in completely different personalities. Occasionally I would have extended conversations with them. Some were friendly and talkative, others seductive, and others childlike. On occasion I would have to call on the "helping" alters if I felt something was not right. Needless to say, working with Mary was a twenty-four hour affair, so sometimes I would find myself completely exhausted after being there.

Judy, Kathy and myself would make times when the three of us would get together and work with Mary. These were primary sessions lasting two and a half to three hours, sometimes even longer. They were planned once every three weeks or so. They were ordeals to say the least. Judy would usually set up the session. You worked a lot with guided imagery; titanium walls, treasure boxes, ray guns, golden keys, beautiful blue oceans and so on. This would direct the client's imagination in a way that would help them. But it didn't always mean that the fragment or alter was gone forever.

I did meet Stanley. After that one big episode at the hospital we thought we would bring Stanley out and find out what was going on. I remember Kathy being very nervous about this. Stanley and I hadn't been formally introduced, though he knew of me through the "others" in Mary's system. When Stanley came out, "He" emerged with a man's voice, and he/Mary stood up without saying a word and proceeded to back me up into a corner of the room, looking at me with a hard stare. Judy was yelling "Stanley! Stanley!" Then...Mary!" No response. He came at me raising both arms towards me. In a quick move I turned him around, putting my arms around her body. Then I took her down to the floor while at the same time calling Mary's name. At that point Stanley lost all his energy and we both lay there quietly. Gradually Mary came forth somewhat disoriented and tired. She seemed happy to see me.

Some of our sessions definitely did get physical. I previously had experience having to "take down" adolescents to contain them, so it wasn't completely new, although in this case the context was quite different.

Once there was an alter that came out grabbing Kathy's hair and somehow was able to get an electrical lamp cord and wrapped it around Judy's body. Both of them were incapacitated. She was called "M-5." I jumped on her and had to hold her down. I was only about six inches from her. Right before my eyes Mary's neck changed color and her eyes became blood-shot red with huge black, abyss-like pupils. There was no Mary there only this "thing" staring me in the face. No warm-blooded...no nothing! Vacant.

As I lay holding her M-5 began to ridicule and laugh at me. There was such seething hate. For a split second my heart went to my throat. I thought, "Oh my God! What is happening here?" Quickly though I regained my composure. It was like a scene from "The Exorcist." Judy in the meantime was trying to tell me what to say to her. What I could hear from Judy, I would repeat to Mary. Mostly though it took my inner strength to come through and to show M-5 that I was not going to give in and show fear. At times it seemed liked it could see right through me, which was disconcerting to say the least.

Needless to say, this session lasted for some time. After a long struggle M-5 left. When Mary returned it was as though M-5 was never there. Sitting there before me was this gentle person. I got up and left. Returning to my house in Chimayo, I took a very long bath, hugged my dog, drank two Negro Modelo beers and tried to find something funny on the television.

Fortunately my work schedule was no more than twenty five to thirty hours a week. Usually after a big session like that, I wouldn't go in at all the next day. I would make sure not to do any work. I would just take a bath to wash off everything and clear my head. Taking baths became very important to me in those days. Not only was it to clean me on the outside, but to clean me in the inside.

In all there were eight to nine sessions that I did like this, three of which ended in total exhaustion. It wasn't just me, but Judy and Kathy as well. Kathy had the most difficult time. It might have been after that session, I mentioned with M-5. She was so blown away. It was so overwhelming, that she had to stay away for a little while and not have any contact with Mary. I couldn't blame her in the least. It was hard work and it took an emotional toll on you.

It is an understatement to say that working with Mary wasn't a case of simple counseling. As one of my supervisor teachers noted, "John, it sounds like what you're really doing is exorcism." Judy reported at one of our meetings that there were trained professionals, a psychologist, psychiatrist and a clergyman in another part of New Mexico who had met Mary at one time or another, and that each of them firmly believed that she was devil-possessed. I could see where they might think that, though I couldn't completely buy it. I do feel that Mary nonetheless was exposed to incredible cruelty. She was an object...an object to be used for people's ideology and gratification. In a nutshell, what came through Mary was all that filth, and that filth took on different faces. In my work I came face to face (and literally too) with that. If I had been weak it would have never ever worked. This work, unlike any other work I've ever done, demanded something from my innermost being. Adherence to any belief system, religious or psychological, would have greatly interfered in this work with Mary. Love was the only answer.

My sister once said, and I found this funny, "I think, John, that as a kid, seeing those old "Hammer" films, with Christopher Lee and Peter Cushing, "Dracula" probably helped prepare you for this work." Regardless, this work required an enormous amount of energy.

Mary was eventually well enough to move into her own place on the outskirts of town. She continued meeting with Kathy. Judy decided to retire to Arizona.

Mary invited me a few months later to her place. She looked at peace with herself. Sitting out on her deck overlooking the Sandia Mountains, Mary served me Darjeeling tea in her new pottery tea set. We smiled at each other, chatted some, and looked out again at the blue vista.

Journey to India

I was itching to go somewhere. While I loved living in the valley of Chimayo, there was a need for me to make some kind of move...a faraway trip.

It so happened that while attending a Krishnamurti dialogue in Ojai, California, I learned that there was a small group of people leaving for Madras, India to participate in the weeklong centenary honoring the famous Indian teacher, J. Krishnamurti. Krishnamurti had been an important influence in my journey over the years and I had wanted to return to India for a while, so this seemed just the opportunity.

My plan was to stay a month. After attending the Krishnamurti event, I would travel through the southern portion of India, stopping off at the Ramana Maharshi ashram in Tiruvannamalai. Bhagavan (as he was also called) was a very well known and well-loved teacher and saint. I began reading him during my freshman year in college and felt influenced by him immediately. Ramana's primary approach is the Inquiry into the Self.

> *You must distinguish between the 'I', pure in itself, and the 'I'-thought. The latter being merely a thought, sees subject and object, sleeps, wakes up, eats and thinks, dies and is reborn. But the pure 'I' is the pure being, eternal existence, free from ignorance and thought-illusion.*
>
> Sri Bhagavan Ramana Maharshi

I arrived in India the early morning hours. It was January 1995. Memories of my early childhood and teenage years in India flashed back and it felt as though I was coming home.

The Theosophical Society in Madras allowed us to stay there for the week. It was here that Krishnamurti had spent some of his earlier years. The compound was huge. In the morning I would take my early morning stroll along the beach, take a shower and then eat at the "cafeteria" --a very large thatched structure. The food was always fresh. Fortunately, I had brought my own coffee since I was up before breakfast. I had to convince the cook who heated the water how desperately I needed my caffeine. It became a morning ritual, standing nearby quietly and humbly waiting for that water to boil. Finally he puts some in a pot, and with gratitude I'd make my way back to the room to brew my coffee and sit out on the veranda overlooking the Adyar River.

The Krishnamurti Centenary was quite an event, with the President of India and the Dalai Lama making their appearance at the Foundation. Dialogues were held for a few days at one of the Krishnamurti schools. Dialogues are different from discussions. In dialogue people move slowly and thoughtfully into understanding a particular question, such as, "What is relationship," "What is a religious mind," to "Can people change in this violent world?" I found it particularly enlightening to see different views and approaches to these questions from such a culturally diverse group. It is not an easy task to create a common and deeper understanding to questions such as these. It is difficult because we hold consciously or unconsciously to our patterned ways of thinking, emotions and behavior. In a dialogue, a moment might arise in which you "see" something about yourself. This insight can sometimes deeply change you.

Being back in India, I was also reminded of how inwardly and outwardly beautiful Indian women are, and I was tempted to divert my travels to pursue a couple of them. But this time, I somehow did not have the energy for it. Indian women, as I understood it from an Indian woman friend who came along from California, are not like American women. Courtship is done quite slowly, involving the family in the process. I was too much of an American guy in that respect—ready to ride into town and "grab myself a woman I fancied," and then ride out with guns a-blazing! So much for my gentle, spiritual side.

Journey to India

One day while in Madras I got sick, but fortunately, only for a couple of days. After the event, several of us from the group went out to visit Rishi Valley, home of another Krishnamurti School. In Rishi Valley the environment was a mixture of the tropics and something similar to the landscape of New Mexico—a strikingly beautiful area.

Meals were communal, so there was the opportunity to meet some of the students and teachers of the school. One such teacher was a young American girl who had been there a couple of years. She was debating about going back to America; for fear that she would feel out of place in a country so different from India. We spent a little time together and I shared my experience of what it was like to come back to America after living several years overseas. "Definitely culture shock," I told her. "But you do get through it eventually."

Sharing my experiences seemed to help, but another concern she had was about seeing her parents, since they had not been enthusiastic about her living in India, and taking an interest in Krishnamurti's teachings. "Unfortunately," I told her, "not everyone embraces what another does—especially it seems when it comes to our own family."

When I saw her work with children, I could see she put a lot of love and energy into what she did. Although we said we would keep in touch, I have not talked to her since.

"Knock knock!"

"It must be Narayan. Come in, good morning!" It was becoming another ritual in my life here. Narayan, an Indian man in his thirties, a kind of maintenance man, seemed to be infatuated with me and took it upon himself to come every morning at the rising of the sun and bring me a cup of coffee and snack. While sitting in bed watching the sun come up, he would sit quietly on the floor just looking at me, occasionally putting his palms together as in salutations. He didn't speak a word of English and I did not speak a word of Tamil, the native language in these parts. Narayan just seemed happy to be doing this and occasionally we would smile at each other or laugh, for some reason or no reason.

One night he left a pot of roasted peanuts. I was overcome by his generosity especially knowing that he and his family had very little. In return I asked (in a manner of speaking) if there was anything he would like. Since he had an eye on my bandanna from the Hard Times Chili Restaurant in Arlington, Virginia that I used to frequent, I gave him that and some rupees for his family. He wanted to refuse the money, but I insisted.

One day at lunch I had a chance to talk with some of the students from the school. When I asked about what they thought about Krishnamurti's teachings, their view was that it was not really applicable in this world and at this day and time. I thought, "Well this is the response Krishnamurti, I believe, would have wanted, rather than just going along with him." Krishnamurti was a strong believer in a person thinking for him or herself, and obviously the students here at Rishi Valley were showing it.

> *We think knowledge is psychologically of great importance, but it is not. You can't ascend through knowledge, there must be an end of knowledge for the new to be.*
>
> J. Krishnamurti

For some reason today I felt sad and pensive as I sat under the banyan tree. The only things that kept me from getting too wrapped up in my feelings and thoughts was the immensity of this tree which seemed to stretch out everywhere with its branches and roots. I couldn't get over its size.

As I sat there looking, I felt a touch on my hand and then a firm grip. Looking down was a young Indian girl about 13 years old and colorfully dressed, pulling my arm to go with her. Without questioning, I walked with her hand in hand through the fields, over a creek and then eventually to a playing field where children of all ages were involved in different sporting events. Taking my hand, the young girl led me over to a large white open tent and sat me down. She motioned her hand to my mouth, by which I

Journey to India

understood that she would get me something to drink. I nodded yes, and she ran off to get a soft drink. Meanwhile, the teachers, I presumed, were looking at me a little dismayed. I gave a sheepish smile and shrug of my shoulders. Quietly I sat there looking at the sporting events sipping my soft drink when a young boy decided he would sit down beside me while the girl took a little corner of the chair I was sitting on. Again a couple of teachers looked at me. I was beginning to feel a little embarrassed, but it somehow felt very reassuring to me, something like "child protection." I felt like a gentle giant next to them.

After a couple of hours I thanked them and headed back to my room. The little girl followed me, and when I got there pointed to the camera that was inside my room. Through a series of pantomimes, she was asking me to taking a picture of her and others. Motioning with her hand to wait, she went running off. Meanwhile I stretched out on my bed. Just before I was ready to fall into sleep, I heard sounds outside my room. Opening the door, there stood about ten girls, all dressed up in their colorful clothes. They were beautiful...all of them smiling with bright white teeth. With my camera I took several shots. The girl gave me a quick hug and handed me a small piece of paper with her address. I nodded my headed in affirmation and pointing to the camera indicating that I would send her the photos. Off she went as I saw her disappear around the corner of the building.

It was time to leave and head towards Tiruvannamalai. Someone gave me the word that Banu, the Indian woman who came with the group from Ojai, California desired to travel with me. At first I was somewhat reluctant, but then thought it a good thing. I'm glad I did, since we proved to be good traveling companions for each other. She wanted though to see Sai Baba, an Indian guru who had become very popular with Westerners. People associate him with having magical powers to produce small objects in his hands out of thin air. I was curious, but not enough to see him--nevertheless we ventured towards his ashram.

Upon arriving in Puttaparthi, I noticed that just about every place of business had a Sai "this" and a Sai "that." Banu and I stayed at the Sai Renaissance Hotel. As I expected there were a lot of foreigners, mostly Europeans. We arrived in the early afternoon, took a nap and then headed towards the ashram to attend a "viewing" of him. Men and women were divided and I was packed in like a sardine. I was already feeling claustrophobic. After waiting for about 30 minutes or so, he arrived walking slowly, sometimes throwing candy out towards the devotees and visitors. Coming closer within view, I thought for a minute he might have glanced at me—but then who knows? The two men from Belgium sitting on each side of me were practically cheek-to-cheek with me. "Oh well...so much for having grace bestowed upon me." I was beginning to feel claustrophobic, and the smell of the sweating men squeezed next to me was not pleasant either. It was time to split.

Relieved when I finally got out of the gate, I ventured out to try and find a cup of coffee. As it turned out, there was a coffeehouse combined with a bookstore—my kind of sacred space! Browsing the shelves I came upon a book entitled, Sadguru Nisargadatta Maharaj (A Great Maharashtrian Gnani) Life and Teachings, compiled by Shri G.K. Damodara Row. This was a treat! Buying the book I sat down at one of the tables with it and began to read as though I was caressing a diamond.

> *To exist means to be something, a thing, a feeling, a thought, an idea. All existence is particular. Only being is universal, in the sense that every being is compatible with every other being. Existences clash, being— never. Existence means becoming, change, birth and death and birth again, while in being there is silent peace.*
>
> Sri Nisargadatta Maharaj

Eventually Banu emerged from the ashram looking exhausted, it was about an hour or more that she had been gone.

"What happened Banu, you look tired?"

Journey to India

"Oh John, huh, huh, pooh! I am tired. I didn't realize that we would stay that much longer or else I would have left. I did though enjoy the chanting which was very nice. How about you?"

"Well, I am glad I left when I did. I found this wonderful book and have just been sitting here with my cup of coffee. Are you hungry?"

"Famished!" Banu blurts outs.

"It seems like there will be some good restaurants to choose from. Maybe we can eat, watch a little TV and call it an early night. What do you think?"

"It sounds good to me John." So off we go in our car to our "Sai restaurant" of some kind and finally to the hotel where we both collapse.

The next morning Banu was up bright and early, sounding quite cheery. After an omelet breakfast we jump in our car and head towards Ramana Maharshi's ashram. I was happy about going and glad to be leaving the airy-fairy world of white-dressed westerners. Except for the locals, everyone appeared to be like floating ghosts.

The journey, lasting eleven hours, gave us a chance to chat about all types of things, particularly about Indian women and relationships. Meanwhile our driver was hauling ass with music blaring away. One tape that I really liked was the soundtrack from an Indian movie. By the time we arrived at the ashram in the evening we were exhausted. Fortunately the people that were in the room had just left so it was available. After making the payment for the trip, the driver rushed back saying he needed to get something for me—it was the tape that I liked.

I was amazed.

The room was simple with a bed and small desk. I noticed monkeys hanging around outside. They must have known we had some food. Walking out I viewed Arunachala (Hill of Wisdom) Mountain, the mountain that Bhagavan had loved so much. In his younger years he had lived in a cave in the mountain before moving to the ashram that was built for him. Bhagavan loved to take walks around Arunachala, so a tradition began with many seekers making this trek believing it to encourage their practice.

This ashram itself was a relatively small unlike the vast layout of Sai Baba's place. Here at Ramana's ashram it was more intimate and conducive to reflection. There were a couple of places one could go to meditate or just sit with others.

During Bhagavan's life all types of people from all over the world visited him until his death in 1950. Also the peacocks that he loved so much were all over the grounds of the ashram. I could not help but gaze at their colorful feathers when they were spread open.

The meals were taken care of and were very fresh and tasty, though after a while I did have to back off from the curry. My bowels were beginning to feel overworked. Southern Indian cooking was a bit too overwhelming, so I went to eating more simple things like rice, yogurt, *chappatti* (flat bread), and bananas. Occasionally I would go across the street to the little shops to buy English shortbread or biscuits, and walk next door to the little shack-like coffee hut. An Austrian who would go on a daily basis got me hooked on the Indian *beedis* (cigarettes).

One day, an Italian woman name Maria, whom I had met at the ashram, and I went to the large Siva Temple in Tiruvannamalai. This is where Ramana had first come and stayed while in deep *samadhi* (state of meditative union with the Absolute) before heading off to Arunachala. As with so many of the temples in India, there were different "goings on." *Sannayasins* (holy men) bathing at the temple pond, curious visitors (such as us), weddings and blessings by an elephant (I was blessed by the trunk on my head with a sudden blow of air.), dancing—some going into a trance, picture taking. Everyone, it seemed, wanted to pose with me. And there were people just hanging out doing whatever.

At one point I entered what appeared to be a cave. It felt like going into the womb of the earth...dark...and in the distance another small cave with people gathered shoulder to shoulder, sweating, intently watching the priests perform a ceremony. Candles were burning everywhere, incense filled the air and everything seemed to take on a yellow-gold appearance. Gently I was moved to the forefront of the altar. Standing there, I was blessed with a colored substance pressed around my forehead while a priest holding both sides of my head chanted. I began to feel out of my body.

Almost as soon as it started, it was finished and I found myself standing outside of the entranceway in the bright sunlight. As if awakening from a deep sleep and feeling quite peaceful, I attempted to find my friend Maria whom I found staring at one particular holy man.

"John, do you think I could take a photo of him?" At that moment, he walked down the stairs towards us and stood next to Maria. Both of us were surprised as he stood next to Maria, as if he knew what she had been thinking. She wanted to give him some rupees, but he refused and went back up the stairs. Halfway up he turns around and looks at me, and smiles...as if knowing something.

It was getting late at this point and we decided to try and get back by dinner. I found myself hungry that evening.

> *I find myself in a series of caves, similar to the Ajanta caves in India, where Buddhist or Hindu monks would stay --dwellings on the side of cliffs. They are not ordinary caves, but structures, carved from the inside out. The rock is whittled around and there are pillars and a series of designs.... I am walking alone through the caves, when I suddenly come upon what appears to be a Buddhist monk, in yellow-orange robes. He signals me, and I walk over to him.*
>
> *He asks me to come into this one room. I don't go in immediately. I stand at the entrance and look at him as he walks into this dark room. In the room there is an altar, like a Christian altar, made out of stone. Standing on the middle of the altar, is a chalice, the grail. He calls to me to come in. I enter the*

darkened room. He takes the chalice in one hand and something like a wand in the other, which he dips into the chalice and starts slowly stirring.

He then hands the chalice to me. I want to refuse to take it. And still it is there. I finally take the chalice, but I am deathly afraid to look into it. Eventually I do. I look into the chalice, and what I see inside is the infinite universe; the stars and galaxies and everything. As I look into it, it's as though I'm entering into it and losing myself.

That evening, I was awakened by what felt like an electric shock going up through my spine up to my head in an explosion. I jolted out of bed.

Staying a week at the ashram, it was time for me to head back up to Madras. Maria was ready to go too, so with a little wheeling and dealing, I found a car with a reasonable rate to drive us with a stop off at Pondicherry, a coastal city off the Bay of Bengal. Pondicherry was once a place owned by the French and had, like the British, left its imprint; particularly in its architecture. There was a well-known and highly ranked French restaurant around the corner from where we stayed. I had read about it in my guidebook and definitely wanted to eat there. After doing a little sightseeing we made our way over to the restaurant that evening which was nearby the hotel. It was wonderful as the smells from the kitchen sifted all around us and a slight breeze from the sea came in though the large windows. I sat slowly drinking my Taj Mahal beer as I looked around. I could feel myself thrown back a hundred years. Even the wait staff dressed and acted as if from another era. For dinner I ate mostly fish, but could not resist trying another dish as well. I took my time as I soaked in this wonderful evening. After eating we took a long and slow stroll along the Bay. It was beautiful...and I could not help but anticipate breakfast there the next day before departing.

Journey to India

Strangely when we went the next morning, it was closed, though we had both been sure it would to be opened. "Well, this is definitely in keeping with India," I told Maria. Knocking on doors and windows did not get anyone's attention so we decided to give it up. Maria felt bad for me since she knew how much I liked the restaurant. Rubbing my back she tried to console me.

Maria was a gentle and strong-willed woman, in her late thirties who originally made the trip with a group from Italy to India, but left them to venture on her own.

"They are a bit wacky and immature," she said.

"I bet they are going to see Sai Baba."

"Oh yes! They see him like God...but in a strange way. How do you American's say...Goo Goo Ga Ga...something like that?" We both laughed. Maria worked as a psychiatrist in Milan, so she wasn't unfamiliar with the "ga ga's."

Meanwhile our bicycle rickshaw driver was entangled with other bicycle rickshaws and motor scooter rickshaws. Everything was at a standstill. It all looked absurd, like something out of a Charlie Chaplin movie. So we paid and thanked him and walked over to the hotel to gather our luggage and head towards Madras.

Arriving in Madras later that afternoon, I found that the Krishnamurti Foundation had not reserved a room. I was upset, but then again agitation usually doesn't get you anywhere except more agitation. So instead, we spent a couple of hours trying to search for a place. Finally someone told me of a place called Hotel Picnic. "What...are you serious?" Life is no picnic, but at least there may be a room available. We snatched it up.

That evening we had a mixture of Indian and Chinese food. This was Maria's last night and both of us were sad about departing. We had become good friends in this short period of traveling together. She needed to fly into Bangalore or as she would say "Bang-ga-lor-eh" to meet up with the group before going back to Italy.

I saw her off at the airport.

It was a few days later at around midnight that I had arranged a scooter rickshaw to pick me up and take me to the airport. Although part of me was glad about getting back to New Mexico and the open spaces, another part was already feeling the sadness of leaving India.

As I whizzed past the little shops with their bright lights, I knew I had fallen back in love with a country that had embraced me once as a child. This was my other home.

The Raven

When I was a child living in Raipur, my stepfather had, on one occasion, gone with the locals from the village to hunt down a wounded fourteen-foot tiger, leaving me alone at our bungalow. In India, this is still one of the threats one might be faced with. After being wounded by another hunter, the tiger was on the prowl killing livestock. It had already "shredded" one man coming back to his village one evening. Needless to say the villagers wanted to protect their neighborhood from further occurrences of this kind, as they were enticing bait to this big creature.

Taking precautions myself, I loaded the gun. I'll always appreciate the time my stepfather took to teach me how to handle guns and to respect their deadly power. Now that I was handling "real guns," and after his training, I was never again allowed, at that young age of ten, to play with toy guns or anything of the kind.

For a while I was content to hang around the grounds of the bungalow. It was a wonderful compound, especially with its large banyan trees that spread their roots in all directions. Sitting on the porch I thought about the local farmers who had a history of having their crops destroyed by the crows. In my own way, I thought that maybe I could help remedy that by going off and trying to shoot some of them or at least scare them off.

Stepping gingerly, I made my way over to a nearby tree and, pressing my shoulder to its trunk, stood sideways so as not to show an inch of my body. Peering around the rim of the trunk, I could see the tree ahead was flooded with crows. It reminded me of a scene from the Hitchcock movie "The Birds." The crows had not seen me yet, so I slowly turned the barrel of the gun in their direction...took aim... and in no time they were gone, scattering in all directions.

The way they get the message, that immediate group reflex, still amazes me. I could hear them cawing in the distance as I made my way back to the bungalow. It sounded to me like they were laughing.

When I got back, I saw the jeep in the driveway and assumed that Rafik, our driver and interpreter, was around. So I went to search for him. Walking to the side of the house, I had a strong sense that something or someone was in close proximity. Also, as though there was a subtle voice coming from inside of me, I followed my intuition as to where it might lead.

I approached a large tree and there I saw, perched on a large branch, only a couple of feet above my head and about fifteen feet away, a huge black bird, unlike any I have ever seen before. I stood there looking at it and it sat there looking at me. At first I thought that it was a crow, but then looking more closely it looked more like a raven.

There it sat there quietly and grandly, like an ancient monarch. Strangely, I intuited that it wanted to end its life. I could feel it in my guts. Anytime I made a little motion, it did not move. I would move my gun expecting it to fly away, but it did nothing. I stood there debating what to do. I mean the reason I had brought the gun out was to shoot some birds, not to be standing there looking at them. The raven continued to look directly at me. There was an eerie silence in the air. The other crows in the distance had stopped cawing—which was very unusual in India! What was I to do?

Then the raven spoke:

"It's okay John. There is no reason to feel bad in ending my life."

"Yes...but now I feel no wish to kill you. You'll die one day naturally anyway."

"John...as you can see I'm an old bird and my ability to fly and maneuver myself in the sky is greatly limited, unlike my younger days when there was such strength in my wings. Over the years my skill as a predator has diminished. I've also been wounded several times by others animals and human beings as well."

"So you wish to end your life sooner because of the pain that you feel, is that it?"

"Oh no...not because of that. That would be too foolish for me, especially since my nature is one of living in constant possible danger. There have been close calls and I've had to endure and live with pain at times. It goes with the territory. Nature though beautiful is also savage. I do not, though, regret it."

I stood there not knowing what to say. Young as I was, I had a deep and quiet understanding of what he was saying.

"So then what is the reason? It seems you would wait until your time to die."

The raven looked serenely at me and said, "There are many ways of dying as well as many reasons. Some that can only be understand by and for oneself."

"So...may I ask again, though I may not really understand?"

"To help others," the raven quickly responded.

"Help others?"

"I don't know if there is such a thing as reincarnation, but if there is, I would like to have the chance to come back as a human being."

"A human being?"

"Yes...it would seem to me that one rarely gets a chance to live the life as a human being. Humans have the ability to create. I would love to create—to create what is good."

"So what does dying early have to do with it? Again, why don't you just wait to die naturally?"

"Because I wish to perform a good act, and this good act may help my chances to be a human being."

"Act...What...?"

Before I knew it, a shot was heard and there I stood with the barrel of the gun upright and a stream of smoke coming out of it. There, lying on the ground was the raven, its pitch-black feathers wrapped firmly around its body.

Leaning my gun against the tree, I walked over and gently cupped the raven in my hands and walked it over to where some magnolia flowers were growing, and placed its body on top of them. The smell of the magnolias permeated the air. A deep sadness came over me and my eyes began to tear.

Walking back to the bungalow as if in mourning, I decided to take a nap on one of the hammock-like beds. For a while I lay staring out of the window looking into the jungle. The sadness sat like a big rock in the middle of my chest. I felt confused and ashamed. Was I just trigger-happy? I questioned my intentions over and over, not coming up with any clear answer. Then I heard Rafik's voice.

"John-soh…are you in there?"

Gathering myself I responded, "Yes Rafik, I'm in here!"

"Could you please come out here, I have some people from the village who wish to see you."

Slowly stepping out onto the front porch there was Rafik with a grin on his face. In the front yard below were about fifty people. All of them were looking up at me. I felt nervous. In front of the crowd was a man holding a black bird, which I recognized at once as the raven. Now I was even more nervous, since I feared that I might have killed a sacred animal. I looked at Rafik who only gave me smile. Seeing him smile eased my tension a bit, but was still considering making a run for it getting the gun for my own protection. Instead I just stood there frozen.

But as I viewed the people standing there, I realized that most were smiling. Had I done something wrong they would not be in a happy mood. The man in front holding the raven motioned to me to come down. Hesitating, I walked over to him. Before long the rest of the crowd gathered around me. Then he spoke in a loud voice.

"I want to thank and congratulate you for killing this bird. It was the king of all the other birds that have caused so much destruction and hardship for us. It was evil in our eyes and now you have stopped that evil we can now have more peace in our lives, thanks to you."

Surprised and a little perplexed I asked, "You mean by stopping this bird that others will not bother you?"

Nodding his head in typical Indian style he says, "Yes...that's exactly what I mean!"

One of the villagers walked over to me and handed over a small box of various Indian sweets. Then hugging me firmly he looked at me. "Please feel free anytime you wish to come and stay in our village...please...anytime. Thank you again."

After shaking his hand and others in the crowd, they then departed to go back to their village. Taking a bite of one of the sweets, I watched them until they finally disappeared around the bend of the road. The sun was just beginning to set and I could begin to feel the coolness in the air.

In the dark night, hearing the sound
Of a crow which does not cry
Makes me long to see my parents
Who are not yet born

        Zen Master Hakuin

Unless a grain of wheat falls to the ground and dies
It remains just a grain of wheat
But if it dies
It produces much fruit.

        John 12:24

A True Companion

Arriving back in Albuquerque from my trip to India, I was looking forward to seeing my dog Cruz. She was quite happy to see me after a month and did her ritualized "wiggly butt" dance, where she lies on her back and moves her whole body back and forth while making grunting noises.

For a while I had to acclimate myself. America has such a different feeling than India...more aggressive, hard, while India has an openness and softness about it. Despite that, it was good to be back...good to see and feel the open spaces and, after being around so many people, it was good to have a cup mocha java coffee and breathe the fresh crisp air. I was craving Mexican food, so my friend and I went out for a feast and downed a few margaritas.

Being with Cruz again helped me adjust to my return. Animals have always played a big part in my life, and being with her was no exception. We met when I was living in Chimayo. One of the locals who could not afford to have her neutered, most likely abandoned her because she was female. Thus the quickest remedy was to drop her off somewhere in the mountains.

I took her name from the Santa Cruz Peak. It was a late afternoon in November and I wanted to take a little hike and have a picnic before heading to work. The weather was nice for walking as I headed towards the peak. After about 15 minutes of hiking on the mesa I saw an animal in the distance and as I...we...got nearer to each other I could tell that it was a type of Australian Shepherd. She was beautiful. Approaching carefully I could sense a gentle nature about her. She must have sensed that about me, as she got closer and closer and finally, after the smell of my hand and a rub on the head we were instant friends! For about ten minutes we stood close to each other looking out at the vista from the mesa. There was a connection.

Walking back to my car I took out some tortillas and gave them to Cruz. She was quite hungry...or maybe she had a fondness for tortillas. In no time they were all gone. I waited for another hour to see if anyone was going to claim her. No one came. Since I had to work that evening, I took her with me and she slept in the car.

The next morning was chilly. We took a short walk and then went on to my home. Cruz settled in right away. After getting some coffee and going to sit in the yard, I noticed strong feelings welling up in me. There was something about having a dog that gives unconditional love. I could sense this so strongly from Cruz, and knew she would become an incredible companion.

I learned from my veterinarian that this breed of dog (either Australian Shepherd mix or a New Zealand Shepherd) was very one-on-one. Sure enough, Cruz seemed to follow my every step. She was very intelligent, and so gentle and kind with people--especially children.

One day we went out to Abiquiu Lake. I jumped in the lake for a swim and Cruz went off to explore. Afterwards I took out the fried chicken I had brought with me. As I sat there eating I began to wonder why Cruz hadn't noticed me dining. She was not one to miss anything, especially when it came to food. Looking out to see if I could spot her, I noticed a head, way in the distance in the lake. I wondered what kind of mammal it could be and then immediately realized that it was Cruz! I could not believe it! Apparently Cruz thought I had swum to the other side (quite some distance) and was determined to find me. Calling out in a loud voice, I saw a little head turn around and head back to shore. I went out to try and meet her half way.

This dog loved me so much that she would risk her own life! Cruz...meaning "Cross," to risk one's own life for another. Can anything be more loving than this?

Now I was back and wondering what to do next. On my answering machine was a message about creating a program for adolescents and their parents, who were having difficulties. It was to be a combined effort of both the school and psychiatric hospital. When I was approached about it, I was interested, but after a couple of meetings it turned out that the parents were not particularly interested. They were not actively disinterested, but apathetic about the whole thing.

It was unfortunate to see this. Though I did not have children, I just could not fathom a mother or father's neglect, yet many were fooling themselves and others that they were "caring" parents. It is easier to lie to oneself, but as in one Zen expression, "the walls know," and eventually everyone pays somehow.

It seemed like it was time to make a move. For some reason I was thinking about Roswell, possibly because of my interest in the whole UFO thing. Santa Fe was getting a bit too much for me. It was turning into "Californication." Almost everyone was into some New Age or traditional/alternative type of thing. Workshops, seminars and visiting gurus etc. were an ongoing part of life there and it would spread like wildfire, once the word got out, as if everyone possessed some satellite dish on top of his or her head. It was beginning to feel too generic in a different sort of way. A little adventure to Southeast New Mexico seemed to beckon me.

So, off I went, deciding to make a loop taking I-25 south to Las Cruces and stopping to visit Brother Stephen, a Benedictine monk friend of mine who was, at the time, taking care of his mother. Continuing on through El Paso towards Carlsbad, I came upon the Guadalupe Mountains. As I was to learn, these are not actually mountains, but rather, a huge mountain-like ancient marine fossil reef stretching for some distance, the highest point being El Capitan at 8,749 feet. It was apparently formed some 250 million years ago during an era known as the Permian age. During this time, a vast ocean full of various life forms covered parts of Texas and New Mexico.

I decided to hike back into the Guadalupe's for a few miles. I met no one on my trek except for deer and tarantulas. An occasional hawk would swoop down close to the side of the cliffs. The air was fresh and the sky deep blue.

This to me was REAL...without the pollution of peoples thinking and ideas. I was badly in need of touching this environment.

Driving on to Carlsbad, I checked into a motel. After the drive, I was looking forward to sitting in a hot tub. Unfortunately the jets weren't working and I had to settle for a lukewarm bath. Still, I made the most of it, and as I lay back in the water I saw the Guadalupe's in my mind's eye.

The next day I visited Carlsbad Caverns, one of the world's largest underground caves, the creation of a 400-mile reef formed at about the same time as the Guadalupe Mountains. These caverns are also home to the 1 million Mexican Free tail Bats that live here from early spring through October and who then head to Mexico for the winter. It's hard to believe that so many bats could live in there, but once I started walking into the caves I could easily see why. It was huge! It was an experience to go so deep into the womb of the earth. Inside I could feel moisture on my body, something quite different considering the dryness of New Mexico.

After exploring for some time, I emerged with the sense of having visited another world or planet and yet here I was now looking out for miles and miles again at mountain scenery from above the caverns. The inner world and the outer world connected by the skin of the earth, and I feel the warm dry air permeate my body.

On the drive back to Carlsbad, I noticed an arm sticking up from the tall grass on the side of the road and a thumb pointing out. I slowed down, but drove past. Within a minute I saw a police car coming in the opposite direction. I flagged him down and told him what I had seen.

"I'm not sure if the man is dead and <u>rigor mortis</u> has set in, but it's strange to see an arm sticking straight up and not be able to see the body."

"Could you show me exactly where he might be?"

"Sure officer, follow my car." Sure enough, the "arm" was still there, looking very creepy as the policeman, with hand on gun, and I slowly approached it. When we got to within ten feet or so, a man suddenly jumped up, scaring us half to death. The officer had pulled out his gun as I stood slightly behind him. The "arm," which now obviously had a body attached to it, started moving back and was visibly frightened. We told him to calm down and said that we had been concerned, thinking he was dead.

"No...I was jest laying there cus I was tired. I thought I could jest hitch-hike at the same time!"

Talk about saving energy! Part of me wanted to laugh and the other part wanted to congratulate him for his ingenuity in thinking of such a thing--it certainly got my attention. I wasn't sure he was going to get many people calling on him though, unless it was the police, an ambulance or the funeral home!

Next destination was Roswell, about 70 miles north of Carlsbad. Roswell is famous for the supposed U.F.O crash. It was after a sighting on July 3, 1947 that a rancher, Mac Brazel came across the wreckage of the craft on his land. Picking up some of the debris he showed it to some of his neighbors. Word then got out to the sheriff about this strange occurrence. On July 8th, they issued a press release saying that it was indeed a flying saucer. Then the next day, the Army Airbase recanted their story and said that they had been mistaken and that actually it was a weather balloon.

Unfortunately, there was only one eyewitness account of the alien bodies from a nurse on the base that was transferred to England and was never heard of after that. But it is interesting that the morgue at the Air Base called a mortuary in Roswell to get a hold of some hermetically sealed coffins and to inquire about how to preserve bodies that had been exposed to the elements without damaging the tissue. To this day, many people feel that it was big government cover up and that not only do they still have the craft, but the aliens as well.

It is a wonderful story. For the most part I believe that there probably was a sighting, though it is hard to pin everything down. All I knew for sure was that Roswell was planning their first U.F.O conference/event and that I definitely wanted to go.

While in Roswell I discovered a state park called Bottomless Lakes. It sits about twelve miles outside of Roswell. Bordered by red bluffs it contains seven small lakes anywhere from seventeen to ninety feet deep. The lakes are fed by an underground spring that originates from the Sacramento Mountains west of Roswell. Curious to know why it is called bottomless, it turns out that it came from when cowboys use to travel the Goodnight-Loving Trail near there and, wanting see how deep it was, they tied ropes together and dropped them in the lake. Apparently they never found bottom, thus the name Bottomless. One friend back East thought it might have originally been named for a type of nude swimming area where you could wear tops, but no bottoms.

I loved the area. The springs and their temperature reminded me a lot of the spring I used to go to outside of Tallahassee, Florida called Wakulla. This water has a slight salty taste to it though, similar to the ocean. I assume that it comes from the minerals in that area. After all, it had once been an ocean.

After spending a few days in Roswell, I headed back towards Chimayo taking Route 285 north to Vaughn. Since I had gotten a late start, I decided to stay at one of the local motels there. Arriving around supper, I was greeted by an Anglo woman in her forties; weathered skin, beautiful green eyes and blonde hair. She was friendly and told me that the local bar had good steak, and that maybe she might go later for a drink. Although I was hungry, it was more for some good Mexican food. I told her maybe I would meet her there later.

Looking at her reservation book, the woman finally lifted her head and said,

"I know what room I'll put you in."

"Which one is that? Are there different types?"

"Sure are... I fixed them up myself. I call them my theme rooms."

"Well which one have you picked out for me?"

Proudly she says, "The Star Trek room! That's it! I could see you on the Enterprise for sure." She had definitely nailed it! When she took me to the room the whole place was truly done up with the Trekie theme. In the bathroom there was a large poster detailing all the specifications of the Starship. I could not get over it, and wound up spending a long time on the toilet studying the whole thing as if my life depended on it.

That evening, after a tasty and spicy local Mexican meal, instead of going to the bar, I went back to my room instead for couple of Heinekens, which I had brought, and to smoke a couple of my Indian *beedis*. The motel sat in the open grassland with nothing around it aside from the road and a building across from it. Other than that, more wide open space. The sun was beginning to set, and the landscape was a soft yellowish-orange color combined with light green from the grass plains. It seemed to stretch for endless distances. I propped my chair against the building and looked out, feeling the spaciousness, simplicity and tenderness of the evening reaching out to me. Small clouds of smoke from my *beedis* rose, and then quickly disappeared into the dusk, and for a moment, as I watched them vanish it was as if I had known them intimately.

Finishing my second Heineken, I began to feel a little tired, but deeply relaxed. Several antelopes shot past a few hundred meters away and then finally settled to graze. There was nothing to think and I sighed deeply as if, for right now, all was very right with the world.

Encino, Clines Corner, Santa Fe, Nambe and finally home. Arriving in Chimayo I knew that I wanted to make the move, and most likely to Roswell. Putting together my resume, I sent it to a counseling agency in Roswell, and to one in Carlsbad. In the meantime, I had a few people I was counseling at home, and in Espanola, group counseling with men involved in domestic violence.

Cruz and I would take daily walks back in the Truchas Mountains just above Chimayo. Truchas peak itself is about 13,102 ft. Quite a tall mountain! I could easily see it from my house and sometimes I could still see snow on the peaks in July. We never hiked that high, but mostly kept in the low to mid area of the mountain. One area that I loved was an open field full of wild flowers bordered by ponderosa pines, with a wonderful view of Truchas. It was so quiet! I can easily understand why there are so many references to Zen priests and monks going deep into the mountains. How the mountain is used as a metaphor for going deep within oneself...quiet, serene and yet majestic.

> *I moved west deep in the mountain*
> *Put trees and mist between me and the river*
> *Old and untroubled I like to sleep late*
> *I hate to hear roosters or bells*
>   Zen monk Stonehouse

It was time for Cruz and I to head towards Roswell for their first homegrown UFO conference. I had booked a couple of nights in a local el cheapo motel and planned to camp for a couple of nights at Bottomless Lakes. The first night was a series of lectures that took place at the local high school. Only a handful of people were there that night, but some were quite a serious about the alien phenomena. Some of their questions made me feel as though at any moment we might be invaded by beings from another planet.

The second day's events took place on the high school football grounds. When Cruz and I walked onto the grounds, people immediately came up to pet her. Tents were set up for all kinds of UFO related things, from pictures and stories of those abducted by aliens to actual implants that had been inserted into a human body by aliens. The difference between fact and fiction was sometimes obvious and sometimes a little blurred. Overall it was interesting to say the least.

As we continued walking, one lady came out of her tent towards Cruz.

"Oh...I love these dogs. We used to have one in our family and they are truly the best! Ours was incredible with the children, as though she was the mother. These dogs would truly swim the ocean and risk their lives for you."

She was bubbling over with joy at seeing Cruz. I wanted to tell her about Cruz's swim at Abiquiu Lake, but she was so involved in being close to Cruz, I didn't want to disturb her.

"She must be thirsty...and you too. Come over to our tent. My husband is an artist and he had an experience of seeing "black helicopters" so he has immersed himself in drawing them." As she put a bowl of water down for Cruz and handed me a coke, I was trying to remember where I had heard about black helicopters.

Curious, I asked, "When and where did you see did you see them?"

Taking his eyes off his drawing and looking into the field, "About three years ago I saw a couple of them. It was around Chama, New Mexico. It was an eerie sight to behold. They looked somewhat like regular military copters but different...darker."

Now it came back to me. There had been cattle mutilations in that area, another phenomenon. There was mention of a black helicopter being seen in the area and a question about whether it had something to do with the cattle.

"Anyway..." he continued, "it made such an impression on me, I've just about devoted all my spare time to drawing them."

I could see that these were "real" people and not given much to fanciful or magical thinking. They were sincere, and it made an impression on me that there are people who have been truly affected by unusual phenomena such as I had in my encounters with the extraterrestrial.

Thanking them for the water and the coke, I continued over to a large tent set up for the ongoing talks. Again it was some of the same audience, all poised to continue the questioning. One woman who got up to speak focused primarily on "balls of light," the phenomena I saw with my friend in Abiquiu. She didn't tell me much more than what I had researched but did recount an interesting story that had happened not long before in southern Colorado.

According to her story, a few men had been out on a camping trip when they met up with a ball of light. Two men fled the scene only to realize they had left their friend behind. Stopping and crouching behind a tree, they noticed an interesting and bizarre scene in which the man, mesmerized by the light, just stood there as the ball actually entered the body.

The man reported that once that happened he had a high-speed flash back of different scenes of his early life. It was around his childhood that one image had stuck with him. He observed the scene in his mind's eye during this event. Deep emotions came up for a while, but then seemed to settle and come to an end. At this point he became more relaxed and a lot calmer as though having resolved it through observation. Once this happened, the ball of light came out of his body and disappeared. Today, according to the speaker, his life has profoundly changed.

The speaker said that although she didn't have a psychological background, she believes that something of a psychological as well as a spiritual nature took place. The audience sat there silently as though they too had just been impacted by the story. Meanwhile Cruz, who is sitting under my chair, perks up as she notices a small dog running across the field.

Later in the day there is a UFO parade with children dressed in alien attire, riding on all kinds of "outer space floats." Everybody enjoyed themselves immensely as laughter and cheers floated down Main Street. That evening a rock/punk band played in the park and some people came dressed as aliens, mostly from the Star Trek episodes. I went for a while, but I was more interested in seeing the laser show at the planetarium. When I got there, I was escorted to one of the seats and lying back ready to doze off, when a lady in her forties with a Janis Joplin hairstyle announced the program.

"Fellow galaxy travelers...I am proud to present to you tonight, a show you will not forget. Tonight's laser show will take you to the far reaches of space, as you sail off to places you have never been before." At this point I'm thinking "WOW! This must be some show!"

Continuing... "Of course in order to make this journey you must have music...good astral music."

"What might this be?" I wondered.

"So lay back...relax and enjoy the show!" As space started to rotate above, my head became very comfortable in my chair...and then the music began--it was the Doors! At first I was not sure if I would enjoy it, but somehow I got "Joplin's" point—the Doors did go well with space travel! So lying back in my reclining chair, off I went into outerspace...the final frontier; traveling further and further out.... When it was over, I went back to my room in the motel completely relaxed, got in bed and astral projected myself to the planet "Sleep" as the Doors serenaded me on my journey.

The next morning I awoke refreshed, went down to Denny's for breakfast, grabbed myself a coffee-to-go and headed towards the UFO crash site just north of Roswell. This was supposedly the exact site, in the middle of nowhere barren desert-like land, where the craft headed skidding off a few times and then finally crashing along a bluff. Bubba and Sherry, the ranchers that owned the land, didn't quite know what to make of the whole thing, but they went along with it for their own reasons. When I got a chance to talk with Bubba, he said that he never believed in them until he saw one hovering over his house...that changed his mind.

I surveyed the area, hoping I guess to get some sort of vibes...

I didn't, though it didn't take much imagination to picture the whole incident. They had planted little flags around the areas where they thought the aliens might have been scattered and I couldn't help wondering how big or small these aliens might have been, since I got the idea that it was not a large craft at all.

I took a few pictures and watched Cruz to see if she would uncover any UFO fragments or alien parts.

While looking at the crash site, I could imagine what it might have been like to see a flying saucer and aliens. It's one thing to see something in the sky, but another to actually see it on earth and touching it!

Whether it truly happened or not, in my mind this area did hold a kind of sacredness like visiting a holy temple or site in India. This place seemed representative of the possibility of life elsewhere, as well as giving us humans meaning; that we are all interconnected to a greater Whole.

Getting back in my car, I head down the dusty road towards Roswell wearing my cool-looking flying saucer T-shirt.

Keeping on the Path

Now, Ananda, in this world, live by making yourself into a torchlight. Depend on yourself, not on others. Make the Dharma a torchlight. Depend on the Dharma, not on anything else.

                      Buddha, Agama Sutra

Most people give importance to careers, educational background and awards and that becomes a part, if not all, of their identity. I have always resisted that. The status quo had never appealed to me. To live and think in that way seems limited, particularly as one got older.

Yet here I was in a profession again, set by certain parameters.

Society wants you to depend upon it and follow it. Religious institutions only seem to follow suit. I'm sure this is, in part, what Buddha was thinking when he said it. This *is* the practice for us to be human beings, not robots or helpless sheep.

We must be capable of living the four seasons in a day, to be keenly aware, to experience, to understand and to be free of the gatherings of each day.
                      J.Krishnamurti

It wasn't long before a call came from a counseling agency in Carlsbad. I had hoped to move to Roswell, but decided to check it out and drove down for the interview. They soon decided to hire me and after checking back with the folks in Roswell, who said it would be a couple of weeks before they had a decision, I chose Carlsbad.

The move couldn't have come at a worse time of the year. It was in August and, though dry, the temperature was 115 degrees! It just about killed me to put my things in storage while I looked for a place to live. Fortunately, as usual, there wasn't a lot and I would periodically return to that air-conditioned truck to sit down and cool off. After a couple of hours, I headed back to the motel where Cruz was waiting, completely wiped out.

The real estate agent called the next morning to say she had a couple of houses for me to look at. The first one was a bit strange with rooms that were connected by little hallways going every which way. Driving around Carlsbad, I noticed a wide assortment of houses; traditional, adobe style, cape cod, English Tudor, beachy, Key West and so on. It made it easy to find someone's house, as they would just tell you the type. I decided on an English Tudor with a large enclosed backyard and three pecan trees.

The next day I met my landlady's husband, Daniel, a sixty's-something, cowboy Hispanic easy-going and soft-spoken. He had grown up in Balmorhea, a small West Texas town. We hit it off right away and I knew we would become fast friends.

Fortunately it was a bit cooler that day, only 109 degrees. It doesn't seem like a big difference, but it is! It made moving much easier and we were finished in no time. Looking at my house, I realized how sparse it was. My first few visitors thought that I was actually moving out, rather than in. But, I liked the roominess. The house in Chimayo was a bit too cozy, especially when visitors were there.

I thought the room in back of the house would serve well for private counseling as it had its own entrance. I had always had private counseling in mind, but for now it was important to have the experience with an agency.

After a few days of getting situated in my new house and checking out Carlsbad, I began work on a Monday. There was the "getting acquainted" period with the staff and then I was hit with all the paperwork, form after form. This was not what I had anticipated! I had known that there would be some writing but not this much. Aside from the private insurers, Federal and State programs paid many of the clients' fees. My enthusiasm began to wane. Over time, the continuous writing and the office politics began to exhaust me. Here were therapists who supposedly had their "shit" together...somewhat at least, acting more in a manner befitting high school students.

There was one Indian man, the psychologist, who had been at the agency for a few years, and who felt it was his karmic lot to be there despite the hassles he had to endure. Though he would tell me of his dreams, he...alas, could not fulfill them at this time because of the debt he owed in a former life. His wife, who was much more positive and cheery, simply went along with it.

I had a load of about ninety clients in all. It seemed everyone wanted to see me. Some of the clients, male and female, would say to their therapist, "Who is that man? I like him...there's something about him...good energy, etc... Is it possible that I could see him?" Some of the therapists were beginning to take it personally.

I did form a close friendship with a young female therapist who joined at about the same time. Erin had a good sense of humor and, she was not about to take shit from anyone. We began to hang out together. This pleased the Agency director who seemed to think that if we were lovers, we might get married and settle in Carlsbad, thereby continuing at the agency. We didn't care much for her. Nothing could have been further from her ideal, since Erin was lesbian.

After about four months, Erin and I were beginning to tire of being there. Erin started to play, or to be "sick" more often, while I kept my distance from the director and other therapists. The office staff and I kept a close alliance. They understood what I was going through and tried to be as helpful and supportive as possible.

I decided to make it a goal to try to stay there a year but found myself quickly losing fortitude. One day, I had a couple in for therapy. Someone had taken one of my chairs, and I could not find it anywhere. I resorted to taking a simple plastic office chair from the meeting room. The next day the director came to me in a huff to tell me that, "In no way should I ever, ever move any office furniture without permission." My attempts at explanation fell on deaf ears.

That was the last straw! I felt as though I was in the "agency of the damned" and the director was the evil queen.

I needed to get out and soon. It was both disturbing and distressing that I was supposed to be there to help people, and that I couldn't do my job without these constant interruptions and dramas. All my good intentions had gradually, yet inevitably, evaporated.

    TIME for a road trip.

Face-off with Nature

Out in Western Texas, just below New Mexico and situated in the Davis Mountains is a town called Fort Davis. I had come here during Christmas and found the landscape captivating and the people friendly. At that time I stayed at the Hotel Limpia, an old western hotel restored in 1912.

Cruz was welcome there as well without the usual pet deposit. The night we arrived they had a party, and invited not only the hotel guests but the local town folk as well. Cruz was free to roam about the hotel and found herself quite at home. The champagne and food was abundant and we both enjoyed ourselves thoroughly. The place made quite an impression on me, so we stayed on for four days.

The McDonald observatory is also situated in Fort Davis and one can see why. The night sky is so incredibly clear there! From here one sees stars that one has probably never seen before. Sometimes it felt as though I could almost touch the planets.

The waitress at the restaurant at Fort Davis told me about a local phenomenon known as the "Marfa Lights." It seems that people have come from around the world to the little town of Marfa to look at night for the appearance of these strange lights. The Apaches apparently called them "ghost lights" and attributed them to the wandering spirits of their ancestors. Early settlers reported them back in the 1880's. Today, skeptics believe they are car lights from a highway off in the distance. As scientists have come to rule out various theories, such as phosphorous and uranium deposits, methane or swamp gas, their origin remains a mystery.

The waitress had seen the lights herself a couple of years earlier, though she wasn't sure whether they would still be visible. I decided to go and investigate, and made the half-hour drive to the viewing area outside of Marfa that night. While the lights did not appear that night, the phenomenon is still a curious one to me.

Face-off with Nature

This was a good time for me to head back to Ft. Davis, but this time I decided to camp out for two nights, and then stay a third night at the hotel. I needed to clear my head and make a decision about what to do next. As Cruz and I drove out, it became apparent about an hour and a half into the trip that I needed to leave the agency. It was not where I wanted to be that was for sure.

By the time we pulled into the campgrounds, I already felt healthier, clearer and more grounded. It was wonderful to be in nature, and as my anxieties decreased, I knew I was in the right place.

It was around 2:00 p.m. when I pitched my tent. Being tired, I lay down on the sleeping bag that I had spread out in the tent leaving the front flap of the tent open. It didn't take long for me to "crash"...gone to the world. About twenty minutes later I heard Cruz barking. Looking out my tent door, I saw what looked like dogs from behind, but there was something different about Cruz' bark. So, getting up and standing there in my underwear, I found myself seeing something frightful - a wild boar faced off with Cruz! My heart leapt to my throat. Not only that but standing next to me were about eight Javelinas. These wild pigs are found in the wastelands of the Chihuahuan and Sonoran Deserts, and travel in bands of six to twelve, although as many as fifty have been seen together. Sometimes they can be smelled before they are seen and they tend to make a lot of noise, grunting, squealing and so on. While they can be skittish to humans they have also been known to charge. They also seem to have a fondness for small dogs. Fortunately Cruz was not small, but with the boar present and wanting to attack, it looked like they were all eyeing her for a meal.

I slowly picked up some rocks next to the arroyo. I tried calling to Cruz, but there was no way she was going to take her eyes off the boar. I tried making noises and threatening it by pretending I was going to throw a rock. This seemed to make it angrier. At one point Cruz jumped in front when the boar was getting ready to lunge at me. It appeared that this whole situation was going to be a bloody mess and horrible dread came over me.

But then Cruz did something both remarkable and dangerous. She decided to go in for the attack. She took on a ferocious look that I had never seen before. Dust flew everywhere as Cruz attacked. The boar, instead of meeting her, backed off and even began running back a little ways. Cruz immediately saw her chance and ran back to crouch behind the tent. The boar looked a little confused and was no doubt wondering where she'd gone.

At that moment, I saw our chance to make a mad dash to safety and hollered for Cruz to come. We both ran like a couple of bats out of hell and dove in to my car. Meanwhile, the Javelinas just stood there, not making a move. The boar, befuddled, sniffed around the outside of the tent. After about five minutes, the "pack of pigs" made their way slowly down the arroyo, finally vanishing out of sight. Needless to say Cruz and I were very relieved and decided to sit in the car for another two minutes to make sure there was no return visit. As I hugged her, I could tell that she was glad that we had made it. Her eyes seemed to sparkle and her teeth seemed to look whiter and bigger. This adventure had brought us closer to the terrible side of nature, one that we would not want to meet often, and to each other.

It was time for a drink. I reached for a beer and most importantly for a piece of fried chicken for Cruz. We slowly made our way out of the car and went to sit under a tree, keeping our eyes wide-open. The shade cooled us, the beer tasted real good and I'm sure Cruz found the fried chicken to be excellent.

As evening came, it became cooler so I started a blazing campfire. While I watched the flames and sparks, Cruz kept her eyes towards the darkness. She was keeping very alert, though I knew no beast of the night would approach with a fire going.

For some reason work never entered my mind. In fact not much at all entered my mind. Out here under the Milky Way that was so visible I could hear the sound of the night sky. Sparks flew into the air from the crackling of wood and along with my worries, disappear into the void. I breathed in deeply and thanked the universe. Not for anything in particular...just thanking it.

But now it was late, and I was getting sleepy, so putting Cruz in the car I got into my tent ready for a long rest.

Trusting Your Gut

The next morning I awoke completely refreshed. The air was clear and the sky a soft blue. There was a great feeling of being grounded with no anxiety and no concern. Today my mind and heart are clear and acting as one with the environment.

> *The World Honored One, walking with his followers, pointed to the earth and said, "Here is a good place to build a temple." Indra picked the stem of a weed, stood it on the ground, and said, "The building of the temple is already complete."*
>
> Tsungrun lu, 4

I knew what I needed and wanted to do. It was very clear...Leave the agency. Then set up my own private practice using the room in the back of my house for the therapy room. It seemed that it was destined to be that way. Meanwhile Cruz was sniffing around, but still being cautious.

I relaxed back in my folding chair and stared out into the sky, but it wasn't long before the image of a big juicy cheeseburger passed before me. I knew where this was going; to the local fast food restaurant known for their hamburgers. Cruz would appreciate it too.

It was a good few days in Fort Davis. The more time I spent in this area the fonder I became of it. I was already thinking of a return visit in a couple of months, but now was the time to head back to Carlsbad.

When I made the announcement, the director tried to talk me out of it, but to no avail. Some of the others well understood my decision and wished me the best. A couple of staff already knew some people who were interested in seeing me as clients. Most of the two weeks was spent tidying up paperwork. This was not an easy task given the volume. It was a reminder of the sheer extent of the bureaucracy. Yuck! Before leaving, some of the office staff took me out for lunch.

But now enters the "spiritual" crisis.

Something was missing and I needed to find out what it was. It had been five years since I had contacted my Zen teacher. I was reluctant to call him, so I tried to put him out of my mind and focus on establishing my own business. My relationship life was not going well. The woman I was going out with for two and a half months just disappeared. We were planning to have a big Thanksgiving dinner at my house but I heard nothing from her. Finally she called to say that she had made other plans. I was dismayed and hurt. There had been no indication at all of her wanting to leave. In fact it was quite the opposite. Fortunately, a close neighbor invited me to her house for the holiday. This cheered me up.

Barbara was a wonderful person and a remarkable cook, having won awards for her pies. I had dubbed her the "pie lady" and any time she invited me to her house for a home-cooked meal, I was there. Those meals and her hospitality meant a lot to me.

The next couple of months were lonely. Sometimes I felt like a lone tree on a desert island. I was so thankful that there was a companion in my life. Cruz was certainly attentive and would, spontaneously be playful when I needed it most.

Gradually more and more clients came to me. Some came hearing that I had a more "spiritual" bent to my therapy, others came simply because I was new in town. I began to see that Carlsbad was a small town where it could be hard to keep peoples' privacy. Once I was out on a date and I mentioned a man, when she broke out, "Yeah. That's my father! He is going through hell with this woman he's going out with. What a bitch!"

She of course had no idea I was seeing the "bitch" as a client. I quickly veered the conversation in another direction and played stupid.

One day a young woman called, wanting to see me for a session. She said she did not have any "issues" but felt she needed something to lift her spirits. I wasn't sure exactly what she was asking, but I said I would be happy to see her.

The following week she came for her session. She entered the door holding a guitar case and a couple of notebooks. She looked to be about thirty with long brown hair and brown eyes, somewhat attractive looking.

Her voice had a singsong quality to it.

"The reason I needed to see you was that I felt a great need to share, and to be heard. There seems to be little of that in my life and after reading the short article in the newspaper about you, and the focus of your work, I knew you were the one I needed to see. Are you okay with that?"

Telling her that I was definitely okay with it, she pulled out her guitar and notebook. Then she gave me a big smile. "There are some songs I've created. I'd like to play of few of them to you."

Smiling back at her I tell her I'd love to hear them. Leaning back in my chair I took it all in, as she sang one song after another. It was beautiful...her words so full of hope and love and her yearning that all of us as humankind would know that love. I was struck by her passion and wondered how she ever came to this town in the Chihuahuan desert. I imagined she might have tried the "city-life" but, like some others, found it too cold and impersonal.

Pulling out another notebook, she told me she would like to read some of her poetry. This time, it had to do with her personal life and struggles. I could see that music and poetry was her way of keeping at peace when things got rough.

The quality of the therapy room changed. It appeared that all of it lit up and there was a feeling of a certain benediction. We sat together in silence for a few minutes.

Finally, she stood up and giving me a big hug and kiss on the cheek, she left. I never saw her again, either in therapy or around town.

Getting Centered

The Lincoln National Forest was one of my favorite camping places. About an hour and a half from Carlsbad, it was a place that I could get away to for a couple of nights. One ridge near my frequented camping site overlooked the Guadalupe Mountains and the barren desert toward El Paso. There was a large rock protruding from the ridge that was a perfect spot for Cruz and I to perch. Sunset was my favorite time. Looking westward, I could see the soft layers of color change before my eyes over the landscape.

To look so far out with nothing or no one in sight is for me such a relief. Without spaces like this, I just don't think that we human beings can breathe as well. It is a reminder of our origin; the place, as mentioned in a Zen phrase, "before our parents were born." Nothing and no one can ever take this from us. To sit here like this helps me to remember; and when I do remember, there is such a quiet strength. The sun dips behind the earth, and the air grows cooler as does the texture of the ancient rock. I draw Cruz closer to me to warm. She looks out, as if smiling at the world, her pupils widening as night approaches.

> *For a warrior, the spirit is an abstract only because he knows it without words or even thoughts. It's an abstract because he can't conceive what the spirit is. Yet without the slightest chance or desire to understand it, a warrior handles the spirit. He recognizes it, beckons it, entices it, becomes familiar with it, and expresses it with his acts.*
>
> Carlos Castaneda, The Power of Silence

Meanwhile, while I was counseling people with their problems, my life was, though simple, lacking in stimulation beyond the ordinary. My brain was solving problems, yet my heart desired the stimulation of inner growth and challenge. The Zen adage of "When I'm hungry, I eat and when I'm tired, I sleep" was getting boring. Simplicity has its place, but by itself it's like having the same breakfast cereal every morning.

I began meditating again every evening for thirty minutes. Occasionally I would chant the "Heart Sutra" which I had learned years before and knew by memory. I would chant the "Lotus Sutra," considered the most important sutra or teaching. It helped to chant them both, as they gave me a strength and connection to something larger. Daily life was beginning to close in on me and I needed to feel that sense of internal spaciousness again.

> *In order to bring peace and security to living beings*
> *I have appeared in the world*
> *And for the sake of this great assembly*
> *I preach the sweet dew of the pure Law.*
> *This Law is of a single flavor,*
> *That of emancipation, nirvana.*
> *With a single wonderful sound*
> *I expound and unfold its meaning;*
> *Constantly for the sake of the Great Vehicle*
> *I create causes and conditions.*
>
> *I look upon all things*
> *As being universally equal.*
> *I have no mind to favor this or that,*
> *To love one or hate another.*
> *I am without greed or attachment*
> *And without limitation or hindrance.*
> *At all times, for all things*
> *I preach the Law equally;*
> *as I would for a single person,*
> *That same way I do for numerous persons.*
>
> Lotus Sutra (The Parable of Medicinal Herbs)

Raising Big Mind

Bodhi mind; or bodhi-citta, means the mind to live with the Way, or the mind of the Way, the mind of realization, the mind of truth, the mind of suchness. Or, it means one own original mind, or one's own true mind, which rises by the law of primary existences. In a practical sense, it is the mind to observe transience and therefore to practice Buddha's Way and to perform the ideal of helping others before helping oneself.

Dogen

That Sunday morning began like every Sunday morning; a big breakfast with pancakes, bacon or sausage patties, and two eggs over medium, grits, and orange juice and coffee with cream and sugar. I watched my usual news programs, "ABC Week in Review" and "The McLaughlin Group." Sometimes I just love a good intense shouting match. Sunday afternoons are usually open, so long as they don't involve too much movement or thinking.

As I sit on my couch finishing my coffee, I noticed that today felt different. My eyes kept glancing at the phone, as if I was supposed to pick it up. Instead, I went to the kitchen and washed my dishes and then went for a walk around the block...and another walk around the block.

Something was beckoning me. As I continued to walk, it became apparent that I should call my Zenji. The thought came as a jolt, as if waking my body from slumber. I knew that if I reached him, we would be on the phone for a while. There is a big time difference between New Mexico and Kyoto, Japan, so I made myself a cup of coffee, and waited for the right time.

Sitting on the floor, I gazed out the window for a couple of minutes and then began to dial. The ring had that peculiar international tone to it. Two rings, three rings, four....

"Moshi, moshi!" (hello) It was Zenji himself. That somehow didn't surprise me.

"Hello Zenji, this is John."

"Ah...what...oh...John! So good to hear you."

"Good to hear you Zenji."

"I missed you."

"I missed you too," I quickly respond.

"Ah...so...."

"I think of you Zenji, even though you are there and I am here, and that time has passed."

"Oh good...I think of you." (Indiscernible)

"What is that? I couldn't hear you."

"I said, I think of you more than you think of yourself."

"You think of me more than..."

"...More than you think of yourself. Is that not nice?"

"VERY NICE!" We both laugh. I realize how happy and grateful I felt to be making a connection with him again.

Our conversation continued for two hours, with him doing most of the talking. He seemed to know some of my questions even before I asked them. I guessed that he must have been thinking about what I may have been thinking and feeling over those years. As usual, he eventually "cut to the chase" and told me to invite him to New Mexico for ten days. I immediately told him I would.

"You can study intimately with me during that time John...a good thing."

"I would love that, "I told him.

"Also, I can lecture for you on the *Biyan-lu* – the Blue Rock Records which, as you know, are classic Zen teachings. If you can invite no more than ten people to the lecture – this way also it will help economically for you and then you can pay me some stipend. What do you think?"

With some anticipation and butterflies in my stomach, I told him it would be great and that I should be able to round up ten people in this desert town.

"Good, good. I will purchase my ticket once you send a certified check."

"I'll get it to you as soon as possible."

"You are great John...don't EVER forget that."

"I won't."

Getting off the phone, there was a sense of disbelief that I had spoken with him. While thoughts and emotions raced through me, there was also feeling of calm – a calm and confidence that I had not felt for a while. This, I thought, is the essence of connection between a teacher and student. Without these two ingredients, then there is nothing, or only a fantasy relationship. For a moment it was Mind to Mind, Heart to Heart.

A true teacher is never the way that we perceive them. In my history with Zenji, there have been many ways of being with him. As a student that learns, takes risks, feels rejected and as a student held in the esteem of a king. As a student that loves deeply and as a student that feels such anger and resentment. As a student with a keen intelligence and as a student that feels totally stupid and inept: As a student with unshakable courage and as a student of weakness and despair: As a student with absolute flexibility and openness and as a student with rigidity and judgments.

All these and more have made me not only his student, but more importantly a student of my own life. Being with him heightened and "fine-tuned" me to go more deeply with wisdom and compassion into life. He obviously was meant to be an important stepping-stone in my spiritual growth.

I wasn't meant to be a person with a title, caught in the web of so-called professionalism. I wasn't meant to fit into society or follow its norms. My calling has been of a different nature. This has certainly caused problems and difficulties for me, at times distancing me from my family. And there has been an internal battle of sorts, with one side badly wanting to fit in with the world and the other knowing it would only be an excuse to avoid the hand of destiny.

Zenji never tried to control me. He would simply put something in front of me and leave it to me to pursue or practice it or not. And while the relationship had its formal aspects, it was hardly traditional. I never knew what to expect. One of the rules of thumb in Zen was to expect the unexpected. There was no room for complacency. It was living with the "double-edged sword; a sword that could give, and just as quickly take away.

Not long after I sent Zenji the money for the plane ticket, I received his itinerary. Included in it was a message from him to "keep looking at it until I burn a hole through the paper."

A short time later, I received the first few cases of the Blue Rock Records. The first case was one that I recognized, and one of my favorites.

CASE I: Bodidharma's Vacancy and No Holiness

Introduction: Smoke over a hill indicates fire, horns over a fence indicate an ox. Given one corner, grasp the other three; discern at a glance even the difference of an ounce. For *kasaya* (robe) wearing monks this is mere common sense, just as drinking tea and eating meals. They cut off people's various currents of thought by appearing in the East and disappearing from the West, in either adversity or prosperity, by freely taking or giving. Now who can act like that?

CASE:

Emperor Wu of Liang asked Great Teacher Bodhidharma, "What is the first principle of the holy teachings?"

Bodhidharma: "It is vacancy and no holiness."

Emperor Wu: "Who is he who stands before me?"

Bodhidharma: "I don't know."

The Emperor could not grasp his meaning.

Exhausting all means, Bodhidharma thence forded the river; went to the land of Wei.

The Emperor spoke anon to Jygung about this.

Jygung: "Do you actually not know who he is?"

The Emperor: "I don't know."

Jygung: "He is the Bodhisattva. Avalokitesvara, bearer of Buddha's Heart Seal."

Full of regret, the Emperor longed to send for Bodhidharma.

Jugung said: "No use sending for him; even if all the people of your country went, he'd not turn back."

I was primarily struck by the fact that Emperor Wu was trying to figure out who Bodhidharma was. In this case, Bodhidharma was ungraspable in his expression, "I don't know." In other words, if Emperor Wu had been able to abandon his preconceived ideas and views then he would have understood. Emperor Wu held a view of what he saw as holy, therefore dividing holy and ordinary. In the world of Buddha or God though, there is no division.

God is not only high, God is also lowest. Dog, in this sense is God, stone is Buddha. It is hard, though, to grasp this with our relative thinking and way of acting in society.

Bodhidharma was not trying to be elusive or vague. He was trying to express to the Emperor to "wash away" his ideas and let the true world, the world beyond any division, show up. Unfortunately the Emperor was unable to understand, and by the time he did, it was too late.

Study With A Zen Master

It didn't take me long to gather ten people for the lectures, since half of them were clients of mine. None of them had much knowledge of Zen – which I felt was better. What one already presumes to know can get in the way of seeing or hearing something new or fresh.

One therapist friend of mine asked me very basic questions: "What is Zen?" "How can it help us in today's world?" "Who was Buddha?" and so on. He was intent on learning.

Of course I knew from the outset that the <u>Blue Rock Records</u> were no "piece of cake" either. I wondered more and more how Zenji was going to weave these "parables of Zen" into an understandable teaching for everyday people. Zen is in essence nothing but your everyday mind. What better way is there to learn but by immersing oneself more deeply into everyday reality.

My basic wish was that people would get something out of it, if only a small piece of something.

I met Zenji at the airport in Albuquerque, greeting him with a hug. As usual he lightly put his arms around me and patted my back. We looked at each other and smiled. After that, nothing was said until we drove away from the airport.

"Okusan (his wife) and Taiyo send their love to you John,"

"Oh, thank you. How are they?"

"Hmm...well...for the most part. Betsy's eyes are much better after the surgery and can continue to do editing on the *"Biyan-Lu'"*

"That is so good to hear...."

"What's that John...funny shaped hills in the distance?"

"Those are cinder cones, caused by volcanoes."

"Ah...interesting shape."

As I continued to drive, he would question me from time to time, sometimes about people from the past, some of whom I had not thought about for a while. I could not really understand his interest in a few of them, until he told me to somehow keep in touch with them, unless, of course, it was just not to be. I admitted that in some cases it was not to be.

Later we were both quite hungry, so I stopped at a Mexican restaurant. I learned that he loved hot and spicy food but had to be careful due to his sensitive stomach. The waitress suggested fajitas. He loved them and ate them all, washing them down with a few Mexican beers.

We still had a five-hour drive ahead of us and I was planning to take him through the Capitan Mountains. It was already dark as we headed towards Carlsbad. By the time we got to the mountains, Zenji was in a talkative mood – a teaching mood. We stopped in a desolate area where we both lit up a cigarette and looked out into the blackness. The stars above were very visible. Zenji seemed pleased and relaxed.

"Hmm...shadow chasing shadow John," as he takes a big puff of his cigarette.

"Shadow chasing shadow? What does that mean?

"Meaning essentially, no real life...no real person."

"You mean like a ghost?"

Turning to look at me, "Yeah...sort of, but not exactly." Chuckling he again takes a long drag."

"Before maybe only the shadow would appear and one could see their shadow ways."

"Shadow ways?"

"So so! But now it's worse. People have created a shadow, and now that shadow has a shadow – miserable."

Again he chuckles but this time with an almost mischievous sound to it.

"Like giving birth to another shadow?" I ask, trying to comprehend it.

"Yes, exactly."

"So, to me Zenji, that sounds chaotic, messy."

"Yes...messy. Mess making more mess!"

I felt an eeriness and a sense of anxiety for some reason.

Looking over at me and smiling he said, "Wisdom is important John...that intelligence will help you. Okay? Don't forget that."

"I won't!" I quickly respond. Starting the motor I grind back into the main road with my brain feeling some heat. It was pitch black as we round our way through the mountains. After a brief stop in Roswell for cigarettes and coffee, we make our final stretch into Carlsbad.

It was midnight when we finally arrived. I was exhausted as I fell on my futon bed in my study and went right into a deep sleep.

> *Fondling shadows and laboring over forms and not knowing that forms are the origin of the shadows. Raising the voice and stopping its echo and not knowing that voice is the root of echo.*
>
> Wansung Shingziou(1166-1246)

The next morning Zenji was awake before I was, walking up and down the hall singing, "Where's my coffee?" over and over.

"Oh, look, John's big toe is awake. But unfortunately how can only his big toe get coffee?"

"Good morning Zenji."

"Oh, John's awake! Good morning."

"Good morning." I slowly get up onto my elbows.

Meekly asking, "Can you please get coffee."

"Yes, I will Zenji. Do you want cream and a little sugar?"

"If coffee is good, then no, just black. If not, yes."

"Then you first check it out. I only get good coffee now."

"Ah...good...nice, - for us that is," and let's out a laugh.

"Yes," I thought. "This is definitely the Zenji I remember.

After having our coffee, we headed out for an hour walk around the neighborhood. Zenji was going at such a speed that I almost had to run to keep up with him. His posture in walking was different somehow, such that it made his small body almost glide along. Carefully I watched and would try to imitate him.

I remember him telling me once that learning from him was at times like imitating him – his behavior...mannerisms. I would find myself doing just that even without trying to.

"For those John...with purity of mind, walking on water is easy."

The few clouds up above drifted slowly to the northeast. The sky was a deep blue. As I lay on my Navajo blanket, I could feel myself drifting along with them, carrying me in no particular direction. Everywhere was home and within that home I could move about freely, unencumbered, with no limitations. And yet it was as if something very subtle was there to remind me it was watching and taking care.

It was because of "it," that the white clouds could move freely, casting shadows on the green mountains.

Two days had passed and I was already feeling at "home. We moved naturally with each other, like two dolphins of the sea. I, usually slightly behind in all things, but yet almost an equal: Big dolphin and little dolphin, him being the big dolphin, that is.

On the first day of his talks, the audience listened attentively, not wanting to miss a word. It was hard for some to understand his Japanese accent. I would try and catch some of his words myself and give the translation – although it was difficult at times.

I was amazed at how Zenji touched on subjects that were close to home for the audience. I knew most of the people and it was uncanny how he would bring out different examples of the case and relate it to them. I now understood why he wanted a small group of ten or so. With this number, he was able to perceive something in each person and bring some clarity for him or her. Unfortunately some people were not able to get it. Instead of hearing what was being said, they were still trying to get what this little Japanese Zen man was about. This was understandable, in a way, since it was all new for them.

People's perceptions were also interesting. One woman came up to me later and said that what she had enjoyed and got the most out of was watching our relationship and how we seemed to "flow" with each other. She had never seen a relationship between two people like we had.

Another person told me later that he had addressed an issue that had posed difficulty for her in her life for some time and what he had said had seemed to just clear it up. Others were still reflecting or just trying to understand what was said. Another person, we called the "Frog," whose face/mouth, remaining somewhat expressionless through the talks, somehow resembled that of a frog.

I would read the whole case at the beginning of the lectures. My "reading voice" amazed Zenji. During a break, while we were in the kitchen, he joked about my reading of the case and then announced, "End of lecture! Thank you for coming and we will see you tomorrow for the next reading." He obviously felt that my reading was almost enough.

"Let those who have ears to hear...."

Of the ten people that came, only one left after a couple of days, because she had to. For the most part, everyone appeared to be getting something out of it. Zenji would tell them that even if they did not understand anything that was okay because "somehow in your brain it is registering and attempting to understand it." Also he said that it was "a great thing to be here to hear these talks and even those that could not be in this living room were getting something. All phenomena is responding to this." Hearing this would, for some reason, give me the shivers. It was the feeling of having everything in unity at this moment!

That evening, on the last day of the lectures, I barbecued some baby back ribs on the grill. Very tasty! Zenji told me that of all the meals he had had in his life that this one ranked in the top three. I felt joy in hearing that.

For the remainder of the few days that we had left together, we basically hung out. One day, we took a long hike into the Guadalupe Mountains and this time I was able to keep up with him. During our time together I asked many questions and to study with him more. He would remind me to study one thing well, rather than to "scatter oneself with too many things."

"There is much to learn with just one case from the *Biyan-Lu,* John. If you can understand one well...then you'll understand the others as well."

I had to be patient, since there was an urge to quickly "get" all of it. This study made me hungry for more.

"Like anything in life John, one should focus one's energy on <u>that</u> and not bring up various things. Only makes a chaotic and confused mind."

The day arrived to take Zenji to the airport. Though I wished he did not have to leave, we had already discussed a return visit in the next several months during which he would lecture on cases 6-10...of the <u>Blue Rock Collection:</u> Yunmen's "Every Day Is a Fine Day," Hueichi Asks, "What is Buddha?" "Rueiyan's Eyebrows," "Jaujou's Four Gates" and "You Thieving Phony."

We climbed into the "Zen Transport car" heading north towards Albuquerque. On the way, I mentioned a woman in Santa Fe whom I felt had used me to get a job and in return had shown no thanks or gratitude. This had hurt me as I had thought we were good friends. Zenji began to devise ways to get back at her and to teach her a lesson. I went along with his idea for the sake of it and found myself adding to and revising his plan as we talked. The tone of our voices began to sound sinister. I would add another idea and he would say, "Yeah...great idea John! Go on, tell me more...wonderful!" I must admit, it felt cathartic. The more we schemed, the better I felt. The situation had obviously bugged me and this was a great way to relieve myself of it.

We stopped at a Mexican restaurant in Vaughn that I knew had good food. Cruz wasn't with us but Zenji pretends she is, opening the back door for her and signaling her to jump out. He does this so convincingly that I could feel her presence.

Entering the restaurant, our discussion in the car had made me hungry. We both ate like there was no tomorrow.

We arrived at our hotel near the airport at about seven that evening. I was glad to know that the hotel had an indoor pool. Zenji wasn't a particularly good swimmer, but enjoyed wading.

As the evening wore on we practiced some chanting and talked more about the cases of the Blue Rock Collection.

Early the next morning we had coffee, fruit and doughnuts and then drove over to the airport. It was a half-hour before boarding, so we went outside so he could have a smoke and look out at the Sandia Mountains. Nothing was said. He told me that there was no need to stay but I insisted.

Walking back to the gate, I gave him a big hug, which he returned with his usual pat on the back. As he approaches the door to the plane he turns around and gives a little wave goodbye, a slight smile and then disappears. With a sigh, I turn and head towards the parking lot.

After his departure there was time to reflect about our relationship and my wish to study Zen. Since my first exposure to Zen when I lived in London, it has always been in my blood. Studying Zen and studying with Zenji was one and the same. The so-called "direct path" in Zen is by no means simple. I have learned that to study Zen Buddhism, one needs the discerning eye of a teacher. There are <u>many</u> levels of learning. My studying Christianity has led me to believe that Christ must have taught in a similar vein to the ancient Zen Masters.

I assumed that embarking on raising funds for the book was one of those levels of learning. Although I decided not do it anymore, my giving it up did not stop my connection to studying wisdom; in fact, it encouraged it. This has always been my desire. Studying continues like rays of light that hit the mountaintop at different angles.

Bodhidharma said to the Second Patriarch:

There are many ways to enter the Way, but they amount to only two, one through Reason, the other through practice. Entering through Reason means realizing the essence by studying the teachings and deeply believing that all creatures have the same true nature. We cannot make it appear because we let it be covered with external dust and delusion. If we abandon delusion and return to the Truth, sage and ignorant person are the same with no difference between them.

Ehlru syshing lun

During my free time I continued to focus on studying the Blue Rock Collection. Reading and reflecting was the meditation and sometimes I would "sit quietly" for periods of time. Carlsbad was a quiet town with very few distractions – it was good for the contemplative life.

One day there was a Native American ceremony going on in town next to the Pecos River. It was a weeklong event with continual drumming and chanting. I would go down and sit on the banks of the river and just listen. There was something very grounding and reassuring about sitting in that "field" which seemed to broaden my awareness.

Now the Zen Master returns several months later. Picking him up in Albuquerque, we drive 70 miles north to Santa Fe. I had arranged a radio interview and a lecture later that afternoon. The radio interview went very well, but not many people attended the talk, and a couple of people left during the break. For some people, Zenji just did not "look" the part without his robe. There had been those in the past who had been put off by his smoking. As far as wisdom goes, I truly don't think these things are important.

There was one man in his early forties who came to visit us at the motel. He was very intent on wanting to get enlightened. Zenji encouraged him to come down to Carlsbad for the lecture. He eagerly said that he would, but that he first needed to work on a couple of cars.

"How many cars do you have?" Zenji asked.

Proudly, "I have nine cars! A few are real beauties."

Zenji responds, "Oh…that's very nice."

"Yes…maybe I can take you for a spin in my nicest car."

"Oh…yes. That would be good."

"I will definitely plan on coming to Carlsbad. Thank you."

"You're welcome." The man gets up, giving Zenji a smile and shaking our hands, leaves.

We sit there quietly for a while as Zenji puffs on his cigarette. He looks out the window and then looks at me.

"You know John...the best help for him at this point is for him to give up one of his nice cars."

Smiling at me, "If you can, try to obtain one from him for yourself. Do you understand how this is an important thing for him to do?"

Looking directly at him, I pause and then, "Yes I do, Zenji."

"Good. Otherwise, for him, what's the use of studying further? It only adds layer upon layer."

I knew exactly what he was saying. One can never see "the light of day" when he or she just accumulates "stuff," either externally or internally. Giving up is a necessary and very important lesson to learn. Giving up only to one's "comfort level" though, is not the way.

I wasn't opposed to having a new car either, but he never showed up in Carlsbad.

The "Proposal"

The Jacuzzi felt quite nice to us as we sat in it cracking jokes. Zenji's son was especially enjoying it, submerging his face part way so as to blow water bubbles. It was good to see them happy and in good spirits; especially Taigi, who sometimes battled with depression.

At one time, when I lived in Washington DC, Zenji asked me to take his son in for a couple of weeks. Taigi, then in his senior year of high school, was going through a "slump" of sorts and needed some picking up. I was honored that Zenji had thought of me. In our time together, some of which was spent enjoying a little trip through the Southeast, I found Taigi to be a very real and honest person, with surprising insight. He told me that his father had never pushed Buddhism, Zen or meditation on him. He obviously wanted Taigi to find his way at first, although Taigi had been ordained a Buddhist priest at the age of fourteen. This was more of a formality in Japan, something like my own baptism and confirmation in the Episcopal Church.

But now, as we sat in the Jacuzzi, I heard Zenji making a statement about my receiving the Zen precepts and being ordained a priest. At first I wasn't sure what he was saying. I felt as though he wasn't really addressing me. But the more I heard him talk, the more I realized he was! I looked at Taigi and he was looking at me with a serene smile. I had never given any thought to being ordained and didn't in fact know what the precepts were about.

Finally Zenji stood up, told me to think about it, grabbed a towel and ran off to the ---- room. "See you lata alley gata!" I sat there not knowing what to think. Taigi reached over and put his hand on my shoulder and said, "A great thing John. I'm very happy for you."

I felt as though I had just gotten married without knowing it. Staring out at the blue sky, I sank lower into the bubbling water.

The "Proposal"

"So, teacher.... Why does one become ordained as a priest?" Crossing his legs into a half lotus and bouncing a little on the queen size bed to feel its firmness, he looks up and says, "Insurance."

It sounded as though I was an accident waiting to happen. Maybe I was.

The lectures did not go as I had thought they would. There was only one person on a return visit. The other few people were new. In all there were about five people.

My friend Paul in Austin, Texas arranged a place for Zenji to talk there, but again there were only a handful of people. Taigi was upset that I hadn't gotten more people to come. I felt bad and sad. Tempers rose at one point between Taigi and me while we were in Paul's apartment.

The drive from Austin back to Carlsbad, on a road that already seemed endless, now felt like eternity. I felt angry...at everything. Even Zenji's picking the cashews out of the trail mix was beginning to irritate me. Zenji and Taigi were speaking mostly in Japanese now, and I began to think they were conspiring against me.

"Damn Japs."

I was ready to send them back to Japan, but they still had another week. In the meantime, another student flew in from the East Coast. During this time Zenji repeated some of his lectures Case One, "Bodhidharma's Vacancy and No Holiness." Though he had given this lecture on his first visit to Carlsbad, it felt and sounded like a completely different lecture. I sat and listened to it as if I was hearing something new.

> *All Dharmas are in one Dharma, all sentences are in one sentence, all meanings are in one meaning. So by memorizing one Dharma, one sentence, and one meaning, all Dharmas, all sentences, and all meanings are kept.*
>
> Zen Statement

I was glad to be able to sit and once again hear the Dharma. It also eased the tension I had been feeling. Although I was eager to be alone again, the days went by quickly and it wasn't long before I saw them off at the Albuquerque airport. Once they were gone I felt both relief and sadness: Relief to see them go, sadness to see them gone...contradictory feelings colliding with each other.

Now I was faced with the decision of whether to become a Zen priest. Though I wasn't sure how or why, I knew this would be no easy thing. I decided "no" on the spot, but in my heart it was different. Way different!

It is said in Chanyan chingguei:

All Buddhas in the three worlds of past, present and future left family and attained the Way. All twenty-eight patriarchs of India and six patriarchs of China who transmitted Buddha's Heart Seal were, without exception, priests. Come to think of it, only keeping up serene, pure vinaya can one be a paradigm of virtue in the Three Worlds. Studying the precepts is therefore indispensable to studying Zen and seeking the Way. Without detaching from faults and preventing wrongs, how can one become a Buddha or a patriarch?

About ten weeks passed without talking or writing to Zenji. I continued though to listen to the taped *Biyan Lu* lectures and to take notes. The more I listened and wrote, the more I seemed to get some understanding. I was beginning to miss Zenji when one day I got a call from one of his students, Jim, who lived out in Washington DC. He had invited Zenji to come out and give another series of lectures. It would be another couple of months before they

The "Proposal"

were to come, so this gave me a little more time to consider becoming a priest.

I still had some questions, so I felt it was time to call Japan. My big question was "Why me?"

"Because from the beginning of your life John, this is your destiny. I knew this when I first saw you in Maryland at the age of nineteen."

"But how about leaving family?"

"It doesn't mean having no association with your family, not at all. This has to do John, with an internal process, internal change, not external."

"Why do I have fear about becoming a priest?"

"Take that as a good sign."

On the third day of my visit to DC, one late afternoon I was feeling tired. Jim told me to use his room, but Zenji offered his room instead. After about 45 minutes of rest Zenji poked in his head to say it was lecture time, and nothing to start until I read the next case. Slowly, I give a big stretch, and then out of the blue say "Yes," to becoming a priest. He smiles at me as Taigi walks in.

"So maybe John...we can, after the ceremony, have a nice party with family and friends...margaritas...steaks on the grill. Nice, huh?"

Sitting up on the bed, "Yes, very nice. You won't hear any complaint from me."

Taigi pipes in, "So great John! Congratulations."

"Thank you Taigi."

The three of us look at each other as if about to give a "group hug."

"We'll have to figure out a good date to have it in Carlsbad, John."

"When do you think Zenji?"

"Whenever you think is best. No hurry though, okay?"

"Okay."

Both Zenji and Taigi leave the room while I continue to lie on the bed for a moment looking at the ceiling and taking "it" all in. I had just accepted the "marriage" proposal.

Entering the Rank of Buddha

When sentient beings receive Buddha's precepts
  Instantly they enter the rank of all Buddhas
  And their rank equals that of the
  Greatly realized One
  And they are truly Buddha's children.

Brahma Net Sutra

When I got back to Carlsbad, I set the ordination date for November, leaving about five months to prepare. In the meantime, Zenji sent material pertaining to the priesthood, which I meticulously read over and over.

Washington Ranch located just outside of Carlsbad was one of my favorite places. There, under the cottonwood trees and next to the large pond, I would sit and read, reflecting on the teachings of Buddha and the patriarchs: Teachings that were hundreds and thousands of years old. I would slowly reflect on each sentence, sometimes on each word. This was certainly not casual reading. An Indian sage once said that there is great value in just meditating on one phrase or sentence. I found this to be quite true.

I believe some people do this to one degree or another whether from a book or from something once said to them. Each person varies in his or her way and manner in which something speaks to them. In my case, at this time, these readings were truly speaking to me...drawing me in further. There was a deep sense of gratitude to have an opportunity <u>like</u> <u>this</u> in my life on this earth.

Silence permeates as the sun begins to set over the distant mesa. Colors light up the sky and the ground begins to cool.

The next day after Zenji arrives in Carlsbad, we take a hike into the Guadalupe Mountains. It was a good seven-mile hike, and by the last mile Zenji started to race me, quickening his pace. This time I was not to be beaten. I picked up my pace, taking full advantage of my longer legs. This small Zen master was hard to catch, but eventually I did, passing him. Feeling the gratification I raise both my arms and strut my stuff as Zenji plays the defeated Olympic athlete holding his head in his hands:

America   1   Japan 0

> *Do no Evil.*
> *Do all Good*
> *Be beneficial to all sentient beings.*
>
> The Three Inclusive Vows

For lunch I made burritos and marked each paper plate by burrito type: Beef and beans, beef and green chili, bean, beef and potato, green chili. All of us are sitting around the picnic table when I notice Zenji looking at the writing on one of the plates that said "Beans." "Nice calligraphy...did you write this John."

"Yes I did...in a hurry."

He looks up at me smiling and says, "Nice...very nice. Can I buy it?" Everyone laughs and I tell him, "Sure, of course, for a high price." Pretending to give me money, he takes the bean paper plate and holds it to his chest.

During these days, certain jewels of wisdom from Zenji stood out in my mind:

> *Kindness means not limit your method or device to help people.*

Today the weather is pleasant, so I open the doors and windows. There's a knock at the door. No one goes to answer—this is lecture time. There could be chaos in the streets, but nothing would disturb this time. The person enters slowly and quietly and takes a seat on the floor near the door.

> *Express your uniqueness without forms; such as in what you wear or what you have.*
>
> *What is the point of studying spiritual matters if you really don't care about life and death?*

Another beautiful day in New Mexico and today we take a brisk walk around the neighborhood. Cruz was keeping up with us for a while until one of her hips started to bother her. I became very concerned and emotional. Zenji noticed how I was feeling and went over to her, rubbed her head and back and just sat with her. A few hours later she was back to her usual self.

Later he tells me, even if the audience was wearing party hats and had noisemakers, to focus on what I was doing during the ceremony. The image makes me chuckle.

> *Don't dwell on what you know about, dwell in what you don't know.*
>
> *Nothing should enslave you.*

My family arrived today and came to the second part of the lectures in the afternoon. I sensed that Zenji was talking directly to my sister about something she and I had once talked about in the past. It's Thanksgiving Day, and my friend Barbara had offered to make dinner and bring it over. It was a feast had by all. I could hardly move by the end of it, so a few of us went for a short stroll along the Pecos River.

Rehearsal was canceled that evening.

At one point, don't have value judgment about everything outwardly. Inside of your mind, don't have your own relative view. That is <u>sitting meditation</u>.

In each word, there is already a concept. An adult may hold the concept that he or she is a great person but a child may just look at them and say, "I don't like you." Child is purer, more direct.

Therefore, don't become a slave of the concept.

One's original nature is marvelous. Not angering means to assume no individual self, for there is no noumenon in the Dharma.

Lines on the Precepts by
Bodhidharma at Mt. Sung

Today was the last day of lectures. I felt sad that it was ending, but then I was in for a treat when Zenji read a short tale from the "Jataka" stories of the Buddhist tradition that made him break out into a long fit of laughter.

In the Jataka it is said, there was once a bald-headed man who greatly loved his stupid son. When his son went to the mountains, he followed him. There they laid straw matting and slept. A mosquito bit the father's face with his staff. The mosquito left but the father was killed. A tree god declared in a gatha.

*Though wisdom engenders love and hate
Choose not to be intimate with stupidity*

*For the father's sake, stupidity assays to kill
a mosquito
Lo! The father's head, it breaks
And the mosquito flies away.*

Zenji decided to end around mid-afternoon after which we took a long walk towards the Pecos River. There were plenty of leftover turkey and fixings so no one went hungry. I pulled out a couple of bottles of wine.

This evening Zenji scolded his student Larry about not taking care of his body. Just before coming to New Mexico, Larry had gotten into a tussle with someone and had broken his arm. Zenji told him he should be careful not to injure the <u>body of Buddha</u> - particularly for stupid things. Larry listened quietly, giving no excuse for his behavior.

Zenji again expressed his admiration of me, saying how kind and patient I am with others.

Have composure. Don't care so keenly about your own matters. By not having composure and just caring about yourself, you put yourself outside of Truth.

ORDINATION DAY

If we just free and forget body and mind and put them into Buddha's house, then from Buddha's side we are practicing everything, which, when we obediently follow it without any straining power, without exercising our mind, will enable us to detach from life-and-death and become Buddha. Who would prefer to be stagnated in their mind?

Shobogenzo:Shoji [Life-and-Death]

Now Rev. John (Pure Sound) Seniff.

After the ceremony, we all went to the Washington Ranch for a cookout. It's another beautiful New Mexico day.

Zenji sits about 30 feet or so from me looking happy. He looks at me and I see his eyes sparkling like a kaleidoscope.

After eating, I join Taigi and some of the others in a game of Frisbee baseball. I don't stay long though since I want to spend time with my sister as well. She gives me a big hug and tells me how happy she is for me.

That evening, my friend Paul said that somehow I seemed different – more serene...calm and radiating light.

That night I fall into a very deep sleep.

The next day everyone leaves except for Zenji and Taigi. Zenji says it would be good to have a change of scenery before leaving for Japan. I agree, so before leaving I prepare some deli sandwiches for a picnic along the way to Fort Davis, Texas. A couple of hours into the trip we stop at an area that has a very interesting rock formation. Once I had taken out the sandwiches, Taigi begins eating...and eating. I've never seen him consume so much food! For a skinny guy, he was certainly packing it in with comments like "These are great John, can I have another? These sandwiches are incredible!" Just watching him made *me* hungry, so I had another one.

We stay at the Limpia Hotel, where we hang out in the room and on the porch till dinner. That evening we start a nice roaring fire in the lounge area. Zenji has always been fascinated by fire and this time was no exception. Although one of the hotel staff told us not to put in any logs after 9:00 p.m., once she was gone, Zenji got up and loaded the fireplace again. I kept watch. We stayed up late, talking about all kinds of things and sometimes just sitting in silence listening to the crackling fire. At about midnight we started to fade.

The next day, after breakfast and a short hike, we head towards El Paso. Arriving around 4:00 p.m. Zenji is hungry for Mexican food, so after dropping our stuff at the motel we head out in search of a restaurant. We get into a discussion about music. Apparently Taigi almost never listens to music anymore. I find this surprising since at one time he had loved it. He's got the idea that it distracts from his spiritual practice. "For God's sake, Taigi...lighten up!" I think to myself.

That evening we went to bed early and woke up early to a breakfast of doughnuts and coffee. As usual before catching his flight, Zenji stands outside the airport smoking until the very last moment. Putting out his cigarette we head towards the gate. Zenji and Taigi give me a slight bow.

Down the ramp they go, turning around midway to give me a smile and a wave. Standing at a large window, I try to see where they may be sitting on the plane. Impossible to tell, so I just wave to the plane itself.

Walking out of the terminal, I look up at the blue sky, the surrounding desert and mountains, and take a deep breath. "It's all good," I think to myself..."all good."

However and Whatever

To know what you are, you must first investigate and know what you are not.

Sri Nisargadatta Maharaj

When I left my job as clinical director several months later, I had made plans to move back East. There had been talk about establishing a Buddhist Temple. North Carolina was a strong prospect.

Before I left, a woman friend of mine invited me up to Santa Fe to meet a friend of hers. We arranged to meet at the Palace Bar and quickly hit it off. Within three months we were married in a civil court. After fourteen years of being single I thought I would take the plunge: This proved to be a mistake. Soon after the wedding our relationship took a nosedive. I made a brief move to North Carolina and then to Atlanta, Georgia, where Zenji and his family were living. It was not long after that my wife and I we were separated, leaving me wondering "what next?"

We got a divorce. Now it was beginning to look like a separation from Zenji too. He and I got together a few times, but I could not embrace the written by-laws of the temple that he and his family had designed. In fact, I was somewhat surprised that he asked no input from me.

I was just not interested in joining a community with such a hierarchical approach. It was neither my interest nor my style. On top of this, Zenji encouraged us to cold sell his book. This reminded me of something I had already attempted to do and I quickly realized that neither body nor mind was interested in this task.

Instead of a relaxed...or intense atmosphere for learning, the environment took on a quality of having an overriding agenda. Being obedient and following one's teacher in this context felt more like a mission for promoting and selling Buddha. But Mike, a senior student and priest pushed the "how lucky we were" etc., etc., rap in favor of establishing the Temple. There was an aura of exclusivity that I was feeling from the group that was off-putting and draining.

My stomach churned.

Inevitably I grew further apart from Zenji. My investment in this venture had ebbed. I was looking more and more like the lone Zen priest riding off into the sunset. My individual relationship to Zenji in the past was the best part of learning, but this group mentality thing was definitely not.

It was time to move on, for other reasons as well.

"So what now?" I had no desire to stay in Atlanta—that was for sure. After pondering the situation for about a month I decided to leave for Jacksonville, Florida. "Beach...Ah, yes...the beach!" Here was my opportunity to be near an ocean again: To smell the warm salt air and feel the surf.

A few of my friends from Atlanta helped me pack. With about $400 to my name, I headed towards Florida and the ocean pulling a U-Haul. It seems I've come full circle, but am I the wiser for it?

> *Buddha sits quietly by the beach*
> *Margarita in hand*
> *"What else...what else?" they ask.*
> *He responds, "however and whatever."*

> Atlantic Beach, Florida

October, 2000:

"Come soon John, come soon. December or January would be a good time to come to Bombay. Stay a few weeks...okay!"

"I will Mullarpatam, I will come as soon as I can gather the money. I will let you know when."

"Good John...good. It will be very good to finally meet you. Take care and call soon."

"I will."

Mullarpatam was the main translator, close friend and student of Sri Maharaj Nisargadatta before his death in 1981. Maharaj, a sage from the Advaita Vedanta (non-dual) school of thought or approach to spirituality, lived not far from Mullarpatam, so they were able to spend a lot of time together. In a manner of speaking, Mullarpatam, or "Patam", as Maharaj called him knew more of his "marrow" than just his skin or exterior. Most others, it seemed to me, only knew Maharaj's exterior and not his essence.

I never got to meet Sri Nisargadatta, though I had been introduced to his message in 1985, from reading <u>I AM THAT</u>, a book I found hard to put down. Later, in 1992, in California, I had a profound experience seeing a photograph of him. After that I had to talk with someone who had spent time with him.

Fortunately, while living in New Mexico, I met Bill and his wife Shirley who were passing through Santa Fe. They were a delightful couple. It was Bill who told me about Mullarpatam and then twice I communicated with Mullarpatam. First I received a letter from him, and then a phone call while I was in Madras in 1995. He had made an impact on me, so there was a strong desire to see him in person.

Here was the opportunity to get out of my existential pondering and go to India to visit Mullarpatam for a few weeks. I jumped at it. There was a need to "shed these old clothes" and get some fresh ones – a fresh perspective.

I respected Maharaj. He didn't set up a temple or start an organization. Money was not an issue. He simply met people, whoever they were, in a loft apartment in Bombay. Questions were constantly asked, and answers were given...or not, depending on what Maharaj thought was needed.

My question now was...what was my priesthood?

The vows I took were important as part of my practice and journey; it expressed my determination for the spiritual life. Yet the life Zenji led was not totally my life. So now, after being ordained and taking refuge in Buddha, I needed to live my life...to fine tune life, my way. Is this not the real refuge?

"Good John...good. It will be very good to finally meet you. Take care and call soon."

"I will."

Mullarpatam was the main translator, close friend and student of Sri Maharaj Nisargadatta before his death in 1981. Maharaj, a sage from the Advaita Vedanta (non-dual) school of thought or approach to spirituality, lived not far from Mullarpatam, so they were able to spend a lot of time together. In a manner of speaking, Mullarpatam, or "Patam", as Maharaj called him knew more of his "marrow" than just his skin or exterior. Most others, it seemed to me, only knew Maharaj's exterior and not his essence.

I never got to meet Sri Nisargadatta, though I had been introduced to his message in 1985, from reading I AM THAT, a book I found hard to put down. Later, in 1992, in California, I had a profound experience seeing a photograph of him. After that I had to talk with someone who had spent time with him.

Fortunately, while living in New Mexico, I met Bill and his wife Shirley who were passing through Santa Fe. They were a delightful couple. It was Bill who told me about Mullarpatam and then twice I communicated with Mullarpatam. First I received a letter from him, and then a phone call while I was in Madras in 1995. He had made an impact on me, so there was a strong desire to see him in person.

Here was the opportunity to get out of my existential pondering and go to India to visit Mullarpatam for a few weeks. I jumped at it. There was a need to "shed these old clothes" and get some fresh ones – a fresh perspective.

I respected Maharaj. He didn't set up a temple or start an organization. Money was not an issue. He simply met people, whoever they were, in a loft apartment in Bombay. Questions were constantly asked, and answers were given...or not, depending on what Maharaj thought was needed.

My question now was...what was my priesthood?

The vows I took were important as part of my practice and journey; it expressed my determination for the spiritual life. Yet the life Zenji led was not totally my life. So now, after being ordained and taking refuge in Buddha, I needed to live my life...to fine tune life, my way. Is this not the real refuge?

A Return to India

January, 2001:

Maintaining a slow even speed, the airliner descends over Mumbai (Bombay), crossing miles of what look like perpetual slums. It's 1:30 a.m. and I'm looking forward to getting into a real bed. But first there's the usual routine of getting out of the airport and negotiating for a taxi amidst the onslaught of beggars. Finally, I'm heading towards Colaba, a section of Bombay that still retains some of the old British architecture and charm – Indian style. I need to pick up some bottled water. The driver gladly stops his car and runs with urgency into a little brightly lit store to get it for me. Driving through the city, I see the usual sight of people and animals sleeping on the streets. For some reason, this time the immensity of it overwhelms me. It's like witnessing the aftermath of WWIII. The abruptness of it is like someone grabbing you by the balls and saying, "Here I am!" I sit back in silence as we wind through street after street of eerie darkness.

A guard and one of the hotel staff are waiting for my arrival at the hotel. After a long journey it was nice to have someone waiting up for you. Once in my room I quickly take a shower and collapse.

The next day the cawing of crows wakes me, a common sound in India. I order a breakfast of omelet, toast and English tea. After a long shower, I call downstairs to ask if they have a larger room. They do. It is a large room with a balcony overlooking a park. There's a shared bathroom, but I don't mind. I'm just happy to be in India and eager to go for a stroll and see the neighborhood. Before leaving, I call Mullarpatam to schedule a meeting with him the next day.

The hotel is situated near the Gateway to Bombay and the Arabian Sea. There is a wonderful café nearby

147

called Leopold's, a favorite among foreigners. It has an open view and serves a variety of dishes.

Ordering a large San Miguel beer and smoking a *beedi* before lunch, I sit and observe all kinds and types of people passing through. Being here at this moment is both transcendent and grounding. Taking another puff on my *beedi*, I stare into the street. A couple of vendors try to get my attention but they seem like floating shadows as the brightness of the sun behind them glows on the surface of the buildings.

A great peace comes over me. I order another San Miguel and cheese *nan* (Indian yogurt flatbread) from the "happy-to-please" waiter.

The next day I arrive by taxi at Mullarpatam's place. He greets me with a firm handshake and a pleasant smile. His eyes shine.

Taking me in the back room, there I sit with a large photo of Maharaj looking right at me. It is a little intimidating. Seeing the huge photo gave me a better sense of him. How I would have loved to spend a few days with him! Under the photo sits Mullarpatam looking at me as if waiting for me to start.

At first I did not seem to have any questions. My inclination was to just sit there, but eventually we did talk, with Mullarpatam encouraging me to ask questions, no matter what they might be.

The gist of what he had to say was quite clear:

One's consciousness is one's first Guru and the 'Non-Consciousness' is the Sat-Guru – the Highest Guru.

The seeker has to abide in his Consciousness only, prior to mind, prior to emanation of any thoughts.

Man is at the crossroads. Either go out through the senses remain individual and get lost, or reverse inwards towards consciousness to the True Life of Eternity.

In the middle of the second week, I got diarrhea, which was not uncommon in India. But then I got sicker and sicker, waking up in the morning sweating profusely. It didn't look good and Mullarpatam was concerned. A young woman named Aeda, whom I met at Leopold's, recommended a hospital or doctor and urged me to call that night. Although I was quite delirious, I managed to call the number of a doctor that she had given me.

I spoke to a young medical doctor who fortunately came to the hotel that evening. He prescribed a "high-powered medicine" and said it was very good that he had come since my symptoms were quite serious. He told the staff what kind of vegetarian food to get for me, told me to drink plenty of water and prescribed the same sure-fire remedy that I had known as a kid living in India...sipping Coke.

I very slowly started to get my strength back, but was not well yet. Then one night I had a dream:

I am walking on a desolate rocky path in the mountains. It is very gray and has a very eerie feeling to it. I am walking on an incline, and these ghost spirit-like figures are passing by me in the air/sky. They are going through me and by me, passing over my head and near me. It is very eerie. Everything is very dark gray around me. It's as though I have entered another zone. As I make my way up this hill I notice a house. I am about to approach the door to go in. I can see that the house has all the curtains and blinds shut. Even the house itself has a gray feeling to it.

As I am about to enter the house, I look to my left and see a deep ravine with a suspended bridge. On the other side of the bridge, is a man with dark grayish hair who looks about sixty or so, a little heavy set, his belly sticking out. He is holding two snakes in his hand. These are large snakes with a bright, deep glowing green color to them. He begins walking with the snakes and he notices me.

I can see a little cave area in the back, where he must live. He is walking down from that area. He starts to go to the suspended bridge and to put the snakes down onto the bridge. The snakes start crawling across the bridge towards me. They get a little bit more than half way across. I am not quite sure about them. There is a part of me that wants to go towards them and meet them, and a part of me that is trying to be careful because they are, after all, snakes. But they are approaching me.

At this point, as they approach me, I decide to enter the house. As I enter the house, one ghost goes right by my head. Once in the house, I walk over to the blinds and open them up. When I open them up I see this beautiful blue vista. I see the mist and clouds clearing over the mountains, and I see this wonderful panorama looking down into the mountain. The sun is beginning to shine.

When I woke up that morning, I was miraculously so much better. This must have been a dream signifying my near death, as well as a <u>healing dream</u>. That afternoon I was able to take a short walk and realized that the man with the snakes may have been Nityananda, a powerful Guru saint. Many miracles have been attributed to him while he was living and even since his death. I felt very fortunate to have had a visit from him.

My conversations with Mullarpatam resumed again. I told him about my dream. He said I was quite fortunate to have had a dream like that.

> *The best cobras have the internal breath*
> *Listen attentively to the sweet music of the flute.*
> *One who has realized the Self*
> *Loves all people and all things—*
> *As deeply as the cow loves her calf.*
> *This is "same-sightedness" or equal vision.*
>
> Nityananda

Though still somewhat weak, I continued to visit Mullarpatam whose cook served me the Indian yogurt drink called lassi every day. A Belgium woman named Katalina, who had come for a while to the talks paid me a visit while I was sick. I was glad to have met her and our acquaintance was especially informative to me as she was a person who had known Maharaj for some time as well.

It was nearing the time for me to return to America and I wanted to soak up as much of India as I could. Arriving from her trip in the eastern part of India, Aeda granted my first wish, which was a MacDonald's Raj burger and fries. It tasted unbelievably good. Since I was able to eat meat again, we visited the Taj Mahal Hotel restaurant almost daily for their lunch buffet, knowing the meat would be safe there. I was very fortunate that Aeda was there during those days.

I made my last visit to Mullarpatam on the day of my departure. He had arranged for a car to take me to the airport. Slowly putting on my shoes at the entrance of his house, I got up and embraced him. I told him that I hoped to visit him again some day.

"John...you have a good grasp of Maharaj's teachings. I hope I have been valuable to you."

Smiling, "Very valuable! Thank you."

We embrace again and I make my way, teary-eyed towards the car. His eyes follow me until I disappear into the crowded streets of Mumbai.

Epilogue

Traveling helps. Seeing the world mirrored back with new eyes helps. Having someone interpret and dictate your life does not.

I do hope we don't forget what being a human is about. I'm afraid though we might be disregarding ourselves into oblivion.

On occasion when I'm in Barnes and Noble I'll browse the spiritual, health and enlightenment books and magazines. Interesting...like falling leaves decaying. They have their own beauty, but soon they disintegrate turning into mulch. Mulch can be good for a garden as long as it is mixed in with the earth. Then the earth will decide what to do.

More and more I realize that I am my own holy site. How can anything else make it more so? If the environment in which you are does not transform you somehow, how do you expect something else too? You must already be thinking you want to be different, but it turns out you are the same after you do what you think is different.

With persistence the ocean pounds the shore wave after wave. See rightly what keeps you from seeing--what keeps you from listening. Endeavor to know.

Expand your view until you get a glimpse of the full moon rising from the mountaintop.

While you live, live fearlessly, because nobody has created you. Out of you own light you are living. Particularly, live with confidence in the Self.
    Maharaj Nisargadatta

Ikkyu Sojun (1394-1481) was wandering all day around Sagano, a suburb of Kyoto. A farmer asked him, "Are you lost? May I help you?" Ikkyu said, "Thanks but I am not lost" and he kept wandering.